PRINCE
OF
JUDAH

PRINCE
OF
JUDAH
AND OTHER STORIES
OF A GREAT JOURNEY

BY RUFUS LEARSI

ILLUSTRATED BY VIVIAN BERGER

SHENGOLD PUBLISHERS, Inc.
New York

Published by Shengold Publishers, Inc.
45 W. 45th Street, New York 36, N. Y.

Manufactured in the United States of America

This book is for all our
bright and beautiful children
and, in particular,
for *Daniel Zalman and Naomi;*
for *Robert Isaac and Anne Robin;* and
for *Maurie Ann, Jonathan Jeremy,*
Joshua Michael and
Deborah Lee.

CONTENTS

ILLUSTRATIONS

PRINCE OF JUDAH

id I know Nahshon the son of Amminadab? Of course I knew him! Weren't we both slaves of that wicked king of Egypt "who knew not Joseph?" And when the great moment came, didn't we both, together with all the children of Israel, turn our backs upon Egypt and set our faces towards the desert and the Promised Land?

Nahshon was the stuff that heroes are made of, and it would take me too long to tell you all I know about him. So I will speak of only two things, both of which I saw with my own eyes.

The first took place in the vast brickyard outside the city of Raamses. Nahshon and I were among the thousands of slaves who worked there, trampling the clay and making bricks for the cities and strongholds of the Egyptian rulers. Egyptian taskmasters, armed with long whips, moved about among us and brought them down with a sharp crack upon the backs of slaves whom they found lagging at their labor.

It happened one day that we were commanded to assemble in front of the pavilion of Membast, the chief taskmaster, which stood in a corner of the brickfield. Membast had a message for us from the Pharaoh himself, and when he finished reading it a cry of wrath and despair rose up from the assembled bondsmen.

The chief taskmaster seemed to smack his lips as he read the ruler's proclamation.

"To you who call yourselves children of Israel," it ran, "hear the words of your master, the divine Pharaoh, son of the mighty god Amon-Re! Because you have listened to

lying words and nursed rebellion in your hearts, it is my
will to make your burden more heavy. From this day forth
you shall no longer receive the straw for kneading the clay.
Go out into the fields and gather each man his own straw.
But the number of bricks I require from each of you shall
not be diminished. So shall you know what strength there
is in Moses and Aaron to deliver you."

But when the taskmaster heard the roar of rage and
defiance from the assembled slaves a pallor overspread his
broad copper-colored face. His little eyes darted here and
there over the throng until they rested on the man he sought.

"Shimei!" he bellowed. "Come here, old man! Come
here at once!"

Old Shimei had more than once been of service to Membast. The Egyptian called on him whenever the slaves
became restless and threatened to get out of hand. Shimei
knew how to calm them. They stood in awe of the old man
and listened to him. They must be patient, he used to tell
them. They must have faith in the God of their fathers.
Rebellion would only bring down upon them the might of
Egypt, and what strength had they against the swords and
spears of their masters? His words were like oil on troubled
waters.

I stood near the old man and helped him force his way
through the dense multitude to the taskmaster's pavilion.
In the meantime one of the slaves had stood up on a pile
of brickmolds and cried aloud to his fellows.

"It's them we have to thank for this! Moses and Aaron
with their false promises!"

At once his cry was taken up and repeated.

"They are liars and deceivers!"

"They have come to ruin us!"

"They gloat at our misery!"

"Death to Moses and Aaron!"

Old Shimei stood bent and silent before the heaving
throng. Only yesterday the same voices had spoken the

names of Moses and Aaron with blessing. Such, alas, is the faith of the multitude—like the chaff which the winds blow in every direction.

Membast whispered into Shimei's ear and the old man raised his hands. Slowly the shouting of the assembled slaves died until at last a strange stillness lay upon the vast field.

"Brothers!" Shimei's voice broke through the silence, "Dear brothers in bondage and suffering! Why do you let your angry hearts blind your eyes? For endless years we and our fathers have toiled in these fields. No light ever came to shine in our darkness, no hope to lift up our hearts. But only yesterday you saw the dawn of a new light and a new hope. You bowed your heads and worshiped the God of your fathers, for He saw our sorrow and remembered His promise. What is the strength of our masters compared to His might? We scorn their burdens and their boasts. For the days of our bondage are numbered, deliverance is at hand."

At the first words of the old man the chief taskmaster looked puzzled, but as Shimei continued his narrow little eyes became wider, and when he ended, his copper-colored face was purple with rage. He sprang towards the old man and clamped his fingers around his throat.

A shout of dismay broke from the multitude. But Membast's grip was suddenly broken. Someone sprang upon him with the bound of a panther and dealt him a blow that brought him down with a crash to the ground. The newcomer then caught the staggering old man, and holding him in his arms as one holds a small child, he cleaved his way swiftly through the dense crowd and disappeared.

I knew who it was. We all knew who it was.

"Nahshon! Nahshon son of Amminadab! Prince of Judah!" ran from mouth to mouth as the bondsmen made passage for him. Then, almost instantly, they scattered to their labors.

I go on now to the second deed which I saw Nahshon perform. But first you want to know if the Egyptians didn't set off a hunt for him and old Shimei. Of course, the Egyptians hunted high and low for them, but we, the Hebrew slaves, were not altogether helpless. We had our sworn bands. We had our secret hiding places in the reedy swamps of the Nile delta, even in the clefts and caves of the Nubian Desert.

But the fugitives did not have to stay long in hiding. Egypt, as you know, became a plague-stricken land. A mounting terror laid its grip upon the king and his ministers and magicians. There seemed to be only one way for them. They must stop defying the demand of Moses and the God in whose name he spoke. They must give the Hebrew slaves their freedom. They must let them go.

The hour struck at last. Under moon and stars the former slaves stood assembled for the journey to freedom. The king, who had kept changing his mind, had ordered us to be gone before the break of day.

We moved on beyond Succoth and before nightfall of the following day we encamped near one of the inlets of the Red Sea. We were not, of course, a rabble horde. We journeyed by tribes, each tribe under its own leader.

We had scarcely pitched our tents for the night when a cry of panic shook the encampment. The armed might of Egypt was coming down upon us! The monarch had again changed his mind. North and west of us swirled the clouds of dust raised by his host, and through the dust glinted the bronze helmets and chariots of his horsemen and footmen.

They did not, however, swoop down upon us at once. In the deepening dusk we saw their campfires flare in the distance. With the sea in front of us, they knew we could not escape them, and in the light of the morning their handiwork would be more thorough.

As the panic among us mounted we received a strange command and passed it on from clan to clan: "Fold your

Someone dealt him a blow that brought him to the ground.

tents and load your beasts of burden! We are marching towards the sea!"

So we moved on, wondering, fearing, with heavy hearts and without understanding. But long before we reached the shore and saw the waves foaming in the moonlight, a mighty wind had come tearing in from the east. It made even the heavy-laden camels stagger in their tracks.

We halted at the water's edge and the chiefs of the tribes came together to hold counsel. Loud voices rose up among them in sharp dispute. But the leader himself suddenly appeared among them.

"Why do you stand here wrangling?" he cried. "Go forward into the sea! I command you!"

The chiefs looked at one another, amazed and frightened. They held back, each of them waiting for another to be the first. Then it was that the prince of Judah, Nahshon son of Amminadab, strode forward, with Shimei, the old man, behind him.

"Go back!" Nahshon shouted to him above the roar of the wind. "This is not for your feeble strength."

"Nor for yours either!" the old man replied. "Strength is from the Lord of Hosts!"

So Nahshon plunged into the sea and Shimei after him. We saw them struggling with the waves, Nahshon supporting the old man as they strained forward. But after no more than ten or twelve steps, they halted and stood still. They stood still in the bed of the sea!

Nahshon turned and faced the fugitives on the shore.

"The sea is dry!" he shouted. "The waters are driven back! Let the people move forward!"

The rest of the story is too well known for me to repeat. When the dawn came and we were safe on the other shore, we saw the armed hosts of Egypt swept away by the returning waters. A number of us gathered around old Shimei.

"The Lord of Hosts has worked a miracle for us," some one said.

"Yes," Shimei answered. "He always works miracles for men of great faith and great courage."

BILDAD AND ARIEL

The great moment had come. The children of Israel stood together at the foot of the holy mountain, as Moses had ordered. It was a huge gathering, spread-out as far as the eye could reach.

Was there ever an assembly to compare with this one? The former slaves were gathered to listen to the Ten Commandments! Soon the Voice will come down to them from the summit like thunder, and they will hear the first words: "I am the Lord your God who brought you out of the land of Egypt, out of the house of bondage!"

But, from that asssembly a certain youth named Ariel was absent, and Bildad, his closest friend, loitered on the fringes, heartsick and lonely. In one of the booths that covered the plain, far off in the distance, Ariel lay wounded. Beside him sat Elon, his grandfather, who was too feeble to attend the assembly. Since the previous day when Bildad, bent under the burden, carried his friend into the booth, the old man had not left his grandson's side.

The memory of what happened that day never stopped churning and churning in Bildad's mind.

Bildad and Ariel belonged to a battalion of scouts who marched in advance of the Israelite host on the journey through the wilderness. Commanded by Joshua son of Nun, the battalion consisted of the strongest and fastest young men of Israel. If an enemy made his appearance, the scouts were the first to go into battle.

Bildad and Ariel had fought together at the battle of Rephidim against the Amalekites. They went out scouting together, exploring desert nooks that were known only to the lions and foxes. There were few in the battalion who were better known for skill and daring. There was no one who hurled spear or javelin with surer aim than Bildad.

On the day before the assembly the two left the camp just after dawn to explore the crags and defiles near Mount Sinai. Bildad was not eager for this trip, but he rarely opposed his friend's wishes. Ariel noticed that Bildad seemed worried.

"Why do you look so anxious?" he asked him.

Bildad looked down and frowned.

"I had rather not go into this region," he said. "Haven't you heard what the elders say? This is the mountain where God dwells. When He is angry the summit is covered with smoke and flames. And haven't they told you what Moses saw and heard on this height? He heard the voice of God in the burning bush."

A shadow darkened Ariel's face. His friend's fears began to steal into his own heart. But the next moment he leaped upon a rock, waved his spear and called to his friend.

"Come!" he cried. "If we slay some evil beast in one of His glades God will be pleased, I am sure." And off he ran, and Bildad after him and both seemed to have shaken off their fears.

They wove in and out among the boulders, toiled up the sides of tall cliffs, or plunged into deep and dark ravines. They found joy in doing things only because they were hard and risky.

The sun was already beating down on the jagged summit of the mountain. Ariel had run ahead and was out of sight. Suddenly Bildad heard a sound that froze his blood. It was the huge and gasping roar of a lion. The next moment he heard Ariel shouting for help.

Bildad leaped from rock to rock like a panther. He no longer heard Ariel's voice, but the savage roaring of the beast continued. When he arrived on the scene Ariel lay on the ground, the lion standing over him, one of his paws

Bildad hurled his spear and the lion's roar died in a rattle.

resting on the youth's shoulder. With head raised high, the beast was bellowing with rage and pain. The lion was wounded. Ariel's spear still quivered in his flank.

Bildad hurled his spear and the lion's roar died in a rattle. The weapon plunged deep into his throat. His head dropped, he fell over staggering and trembling, and then lay motionless.

Bildad bound his friend's wound, but could not bring him back to consciousness. Through the glades and over the sand heaps, in the blazing heat of the midday sun, he carried his friend back to the encampment.

And since then Ariel had lain on a pile of sheepskins in his father's booth, with old Elon sitting and sometimes dozing at his side.

"I am to blame," Bildad kept saying to himself. "I should not have let him go prying into this strange mountain. They warned me against it. Had I said No, and stood my ground, this would not have happened. We were punished by the God of Moses for running wild through the sacred ground."

Bildad was hardly aware of the people, hushed and silent, before the holy mountain. He had no heart to move forward and stand with the leader of his battalion.

Old Elon started suddenly from his doze. On his ears fell a sound, loud and clear. It was the blast of a ram's horn, breaking the stillness of the morning air like a bugle call.

The old man opened his eyes and cried out with joy. Ariel was sitting up.

"What is the meaning of the ram's horn?" the youth said.

"The people are assembled before the Mount as Moses commanded," the old man answered.

Ariel passed his hands over his eyes, trying hard to remember.

"Where is Bildad?" he asked.

"He too must be there," said Elon.

Ariel rose to his feet, staggering and nearly falling.

"What are we doing here, grandfather?" he said. "Let us go."

They put on clean garments and left the booth together.

Again the ram's horn pealed from the mountain across the desert.

Not far from the fringe of the assembly Ariel stopped, too weak to go on alone. Old Elon, himself hardly able to walk, tried to support him.

But suddenly a stronger arm came to his support. Bildad had run forward and embraced him. "You have come! You are healed!" he cried.

"I heard the call," Ariel answered.

They made their way together through the silent multitude, and took their station beside Joshua son of Nun.

Peal after peal of thunder rolled from the summit of the mount. Clouds of smoke belched upwards, lit up by flashes of lightning. And the Words that will always ring in the hearts of men fell on the ears of the vast assembly.

THE RIVER JORDAN

1.

etonim was a sleepy little town in the territory of the tribe of Gad east of the Jordan River. But on this bright day of spring the town was wide-awake and swarming with people.

The elders of the tribe were assembled in Betonim, together with the captains of Gad's warriors. The armed men of Gad were now ready to march south and join the other battalions of the children of Israel for the conquest of the land on the other side of the River. The leaders of the tribe had come together to make sure that everything was in order for the great adventure.

In the broad square inside the gate of Betonim, Joel, the chief of the tribe, was speaking to the elders and captains. He was a sturdy old man and his firm voice rose above the steady hum of the crowd that moved in and out through the gate.

"Elders and captains of Gad!" Joel spoke. "Let it be our pride and our glory that our tribe has never broken its word. When we received our portion on this side of the Jordan we gave our word that when the other tribes crossed the River to conquer their portions, our armed men would march with them against the enemy. Now the other tribes are ready to cross over, and our warriors are ready to march south and join them. Captains of Gad, have you mustered your men and divided them into companies, large and small?"

"We have!" came the ringing answer of the captains.

"Are your men well provided with shields and spears, bows and darts and other weapons of war?"

"They are!" came the answer.

"Have they been trained to use these weapons with daring and skill?"

"They have!"

"Well done, captains of Gad!" The chief elder bowed his head towards them. "So you may depart and lead your men to Joshua son of Nun, who commands the entire host of Israel. And now I turn to you, elders of Gad," Joel continued. "The bravest and strongest of our tribe are departing, nor can we say how many of them will be spared and when they will return. Elders of Gad, have you seen to it that the lands and herds of every father's house will be cared for in their absence?"

"We have," came the solemn reply of the elders.

"Have you sifted and judged and allowed such to remain in field or pasture as could not be spared from their labor?"

"We have!" the answer was repeated.

"Elders of Gad! Have you made provision for widows and orphans?"

"We have!"

"We are ready now to hear those of our people who may have petitions to lay before us," the chief elder resumed. "If there be any let them come forward and speak."

One after another men and women came forward and bowed before the assembly. They were old men who begged that a son be spared from the fighting host for the labor of the field or vineyard. They were young women who pleaded that their husbands be spared to care for farmstead and household. Each case was speedily disposed of or entrusted to the local elder for further consideration.

By now the sun had wheeled beyond the Jordan towards its setting in the Western Sea. The chief elder was about to declare the session closed. Suddenly a commotion sprang up near the gate. An old woman bestriding a donkey rode rapidly through the crowd, amid the clamor of those who were forced to make way for her. She dismounted near the chief elder and stood before him wringing her hands.

"Who are you and why do you come here in this unseemly manner?" Joel demanded.

"I crave your pardon," the woman answered. "I have ridden since the dawn all the way from Succoth near the border of Manasseh, that you may judge between me and my two sons. They are all I have since my husband fell in battle when Israel fought against Og, king of Bashan.

"My sons, Talmon and Abdiel, are twins and each of them swears that he will be the one to march with the warriors of Gad, and the other must stay behind and tend the flocks and comfort my old age. 'I am the first born and I will go,' says Talmon. 'Since you are the elder, you should stay with our mother,' says Abdiel. They were always knit together in love, but now, alas, there is enmity between them. The clamor of their strife rings in my ears, and day and night I weep for my sons. I pray you, therefore, to judge between them, and I will carry your judgment to them."

The woman ended, tears streaming down her hollow cheeks.

The elders and captains were silent. The din in the square was hushed. The story of this unhappy mother was so strange, her petition so different from the others.

Joel beckoned to three of the other elders and when they had whispered together awhile the chief elder spoke as follows:

"It is clear that both Talmon and Abdiel hold it an honor, greatly to be prized and cherished, to march with the warriors of Gad. And since this honor can fall to only one of them, our ancient laws require that the elder son should have it. We judge therefore that Talmon should be chosen. Are you agreed?"

"Agreed!" the elders and captains replied in a single voice.

2.

There was no rest for Abdiel after his brother's departure. It was not the extra labor which weighed him down. His mother, in fact, had hired some one to help him, a big-boned and gnarled old fellow with the strength of two ordinary men. It was the bitterness in his soul at the judgment of the elders. The decision was unjust, Abdiel kept saying to himself, and his brother had done him a great wrong.

When Talmon was embracing his mother before departing, Abdiel was hiding in one of the sheepfolds. He was too full of anger to bless his brother and bid him farewell. Talmon looked for him and, not finding him, he went away with a heavy heart and a feeling of guilt.

Two days later Abdiel spoke to Guni, the helper whom his mother had hired, and said to him:

"I am going away for several days, and I leave you here alone to care for the sheep and the husbandry. The sheep are shorn and the folds are in good repair. You are strong and faithful, Guni, I know I can trust you. Tell my mother that in three days I'll be home again."

And where was Abdiel going with his shield and spear without saying farewell to his mother? He knew that the warriors of the nation were assembled on the broad plain east of the Jordan opposite Jericho. He knew they were ready and poised to cross over and strike the first blow for the land west of the River. He must take part in this battle! In this battle only. Then he would return and be at peace.

He left just after dawn, and moving rapidly through the paths of the jungles in the Jordan Valley, he spied in the distance the broad plain which was his goal. The plain was deserted! There was no stir of man or beast, and not a single tent was standing.

He ran the rest of the way, but by the time he reached the plain night had fallen. He gazed upon the emptiness around him, puzzled and disheartened. Then he noted some figures bending low and moving about stealthily. He knew they were people of the land, rummaging for whatever the invaders might have left behind. He seized one of them and shook him in his powerful grip.

"Where are they?" he rasped. 'Where is the host of the children of Israel?"

Through his chattering teeth the man managed to answer:

"Over! This morning they crossed over—all of them. Look yonder! Their campfires are burning."

Abdiel released the man who made off like a frightened hare. Then he strode on to the edge of the Jordan. The River flowed black and broad, its current swift, as though impatient and angry.

"This Jordan acts as if it, too, had been held against its will and finally released," was the strange thought that flashed through his mind. Then without losing another moment he swung his shield around behind him, grasped his spear firmly and plunged into the swift current.

3.

In the plain of Gilgal, where the warriors of Israel were now encamped, the fires had burned down and the men were asleep in their tents. But Talmon was too restless to sleep. He sat on the ground near the flap of his tent listening to the faint stirrings of the camp in the heavy stillness. Off to the west loomed the walls and turrets of Jericho, a dark and silent city. It seemed to be waiting, numb and helpless as in a dream, for the doom which was about to strike her.

The men laid their burden at Talmon's feet.

But Talmon was thinking about his brother Abdiel. Was he asleep now, or was he also awake, too sullen and bitter to sleep? Had he, Talmon, done the right thing? His claim, of course, had been upheld by the elders. But should he not have yielded it to his brother after all? It was lonely without him. And how it hurt to think he was unhappy, and his own brother the cause of it!

The stillness was suddenly broken by voices and the tread of heavy feet. As they approached he heard his own name:

"Talmon! Talmon of Gad!"

He answered, and four men came forward carrying a burden which they laid at his feet.

"Abdiel!" cried Talmon bending over his brother.

"We were on sentinel duty near the river," one of the men explained. "This man staggered out of the water and fell down on the bank. When we reached him all he could say was 'Talmon, Gad!' Then he fainted or died, we don't know which."

Abdiel was not dead, but it was quite awhile before Talmon revived him. The brothers embraced and wept together.

"Take my place here, Abdiel," said Talmon, "I'll go back to our flocks."

"No," said Abdiel. "Now my heart is cleansed, my thoughts are clear. The waters of the Jordan have healed me. The judgment of the elders was just. At dawn I go back to our mother. No," he added smiling, "I'll not trust myself to this angry river again. I'll make my way through the valley up to the ford opposite Zarethan, which you and I know well."

At dawn the two brothers, Talmon and Abdiel, embraced again and parted, each one to his own task.

A KING IS CROWNED

From the hilltop where her father had left her Huldah looked down on the broad meadow below and caught her breath. Never in the eleven years of her life had she seen such a huge throng of people.

"The children of Israel have all come here for the crowning of the king," said she to herself.

The children of Israel were not, of course, all there. Far from it. The people in general remained in their villages and towns, plying their crafts, tilling their fields, shepherding their flocks and tending their vineyards and olive groves. Only the elders of the tribes and the chiefs of the larger clans had come to Mizpah at the call of Samuel, their prophet and leader. Besides, women were altogether absent, for in those days it was not thought proper for women to take part in public affairs. That, indeed, was the reason why her father had taken Huldah to the hill, from where she would have an excellent view of the spectacle.

But to the little maid, who had never before been away from her native village in the far north, it seemed as if the entire nation was assembled to witness the crowning of the first king of Israel.

Her father took the long journey because he was the chief elder of the tribe of Zebulun, and he took his little daughter along because he was not willing to be parted from her for nearly a week. He doted on his little girl. She was the child of his old age and he had seen all his other children come to an untimely end.

So for the first time in her life Huldah had left her

village and journeyed through the land with her father
and his servants. It was a journey filled with wonder and
delight. Every new vista seemed more beautiful than the
others. Every object and event became a sort of marvel.

The high ground where her father left her was covered
with vehicles and other belongings of the men who had
come from distant places. Farther off stood a large knot of
donkeys, oxen and camels, munching their fodder. To the
south rose and fell the round green summits of Benjamin,
and the rugged hills of Ephraim rolled away to the north.
But Huldah's eyes were riveted on the great assembly
below her. Facing her at the further end stood the chief
elders of the tribe, and with a thrill of pride she recognized
her father among them.

But suddenly she heard a sound of footsteps behind her,
and when she turned she stood face to face with a stranger.
He was very tall and his shoulders were broad, but the
face that looked down upon her was the face of a youth.
His cheeks were covered with a soft down, his lips were
curved in a wisp of a smile and there was a gleam of
amusement in his deep eyes. "What a beautiful face!" was
the first though in Huldah's mind. "Beautiful, and also
sad," she added.

From the first moment she felt entirely at ease with the
stranger.

"What are you doing up here?" she asked him. "You
should be down below with the other men."

"Perhaps I should," he answered. "But from here the
view is much better. Don't you agree?"

"Yes, but I can't hear very much."

"You don't have to. I know what they are saying and
I'll tell you."

Huldah went off into a ripple of silvery laughter.

"How can you know if you don't hear them?" she demanded.

"But I know. I know in advance," he assured her.

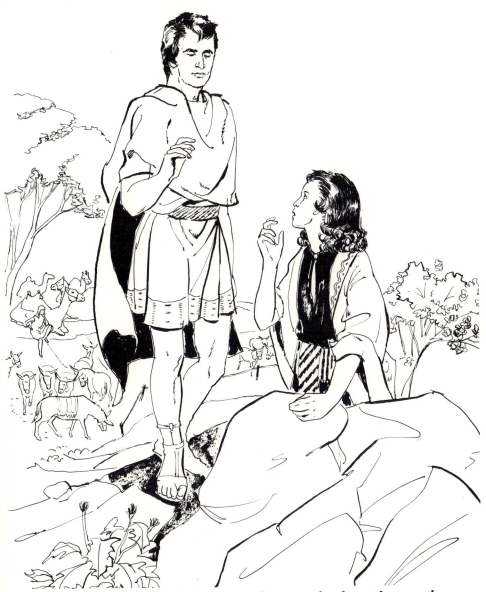

The face that looked down upon her was the face of a youth.

Her face became serious.

"Very well. I'll put you to the test," she said. "Who is that tall man with the white beard and what is he saying?"

"It's the prophet Samuel, and he is warning the people against choosing a king."

"Now I see that you are making fun of me," she replied with a touch of anger. "Wasn't it Samuel himself who called the elders to come here and choose a king?"

"Yes, but he didn't do it gladly. The people said they must have a king to unite the tribes against their enemies and Samuel had to grant them their wish. But he was not happy to do it. So now, before they choose the king, he is telling them what they may expect."

Huldah was impressed. "What is he saying?" she whispered.

"He is saying that the king may become their master and they will be his slaves. The king will take their sons to fight for him and their daughters to toil for him in his palace. He will take away part of their crops, their cattle and their beasts of burden. Then they will be sorry they ever asked for a king to reign over them."

Huldah listened to him with growing wonder.

"But how do you know all that, since you can't hear him any more than I can?" she finally demanded.

"You see," he told her, "I have heard him say these things before, and he told me he would repeat them at this assembly, that the people may know them and take them to heart."

"Samuel himself told you? In that case, you must know him!"

"I do indeed," he replied.

"You are surely an important person," she continued. "Perhaps you also know the man who will be chosen king."

"Yes, him too," said the youth, and there was a deeper note of sadness in his voice.

"Tell me, then," she begged him. "Is he really good and brave and strong and wise, as my father says he must be?"

"All that?" the youth smiled. "Hardly, I am afraid. Besides, he is too young."

"But you, too, are young," she smiled back at him. "Is he younger than you?"

"No. We are the same age."

"Are you, perhaps, friends? Good friends?"

"Well," he said, and his smile changed to a laugh. "We are pretty close, but not always good friends."

"So what sort of man is he?" she insisted.

"Just a simple lad," he replied and his voice became sad again. "A shepherd and plowboy, tending his father's sheep and plowing his father's fields."

She was silent awhile and then said:

"Shall I tell you what I think? The king of Israel should be someone who is older and more important. Don't you agree?"

"I do, indeed!" he replied eagerly. "And I can tell you" he added, smiling again, "that he himself would also agree."

"Nevertheless," she said, "he must be proud to be the king."

"No, no," he answered. "He is not proud. The truth is that he is afraid. He knows how hard it will be to reign over his people, with so many enemies around them, and they themselves not united. And he doubts very much if he is the right man to wear the crown."

"In that case," she mused, "he cannot be happy."

"You are right," he answered, his voice now softer and sadder. "He is very unhappy."

She looked up at him and was startled to see a tear break from the corner of his eyes and roll down his cheek. With a sudden impulse she took his hand and pressed it.

"He must be very dear to you, this friend," she whispered.

But at that moment the sound of a number of voices fell on their ears. The voices came nearer and the words became distinct.

"Saul son of Kish!" they called. "Saul of Benjamin! Come out of your hiding place! Come down into the assembly! Samuel commands it!"

The youth drew himself up and quivered as if an electric shock had passed through him. Then, swiftly, he lifted up the little girl, planted a kiss on each one of her cheeks, and set her down again.

Huldah was startled. But she was even more startled by the sudden change which had come over him. He seemed to have grown still taller, his shoulders still broader. His expression was no longer vague and sad. It was calm and commanding.

Three men appeared and stood before him with bowed heads. The youth strode past them with the proud tread of a monarch. The three men followed him and all four disappeared.

In a few moments Huldah saw them again. They were now on the fringe of the assembly, the youth striding proudly forward, the three men following close behind. Hastily the throng divided to make passage for them. Huldah saw the youth move towards the group of elders at the farther end, and halt before the aged prophet. She saw him bend as Samuel poured oil on his head. Then she heard a deafening shout. Again and again it was repeated and the words became distinct.

"Long live the king!" the vast assembly shouted.

She was still in a daze when, sometime later, her father sought her out. She roused herself and ran to meet him. The elder was still deeply moved. He took her in his arms and kissed her on the head. But she laid her head on his breast and burst into sobbing.

"What is it, child? What is it?" he asked her anxiously.

"The king, father, the poor king!" she managed to say between her sobs. "He— he is so wonderful, father! But he is unhappy. So very, very unhappy!"

FLIGHT AND RETURN

1.

After a weary journey over the hills and hollows of Judah, Eliphal came at last to Adullam. But it was no simple matter to be admitted into the band of men who held this cave and fortress.

He found himself facing three rugged giants with tousled locks and beards, who asked him questions.

"So you want to be one of David's men, do you?" said the one in the middle, who seemed to be their chief.

"I do, in all faith," Eliphal replied.

"And will you tell us why?"

"Because David is fighting the Philistines."

"That's not what I want to know," said the shaggy giant grimly. "We here in Adullam don't care what grudges our men bear in their hearts, or what debts they owe. I want to know what strength is in you and what skill do you have that would give you the right to be one of David's followers."

"I can hurl spear and javelin without missing the mark," said Eliphal. "I know how to bend the bow and speed the arrow to its goal, and I can thrust and parry with the long dagger as well as any man."

"So!" the hairy one growled. "You are quite a fellow, if I am to judge by your words. And what if there should be neither spear nor bow nor dagger in your hands?"

"Then I rely on the strength of my arms," said Eliphal.

"Did you hear that, Igal?" the questioner turned to one of his companions. "This lad has strength in his arms."

In a twinkling Igal seized Eliphal by the wrist, jerked him forward and flung him over his shoulder to the ground. Eliphal landed on his back, astonished and dazed.

A roar of delight went up from the others, in which they were joined by more of David's guerrillas.

Slowly Eliphal rose to his feet, but before he was firmly planted Igal repeated the maneuver. The laughter was now louder and heartier. Eliphal stood up and was brought down a third time. The onlookers, who now formed a large group, bent over with laughter and slapped each other's backs with delight.

"That's enough, Igal," said the hairy one. "The lad will rest awhile on the ground."

But Eliphal had sat up, then rose to a crouching position. The two men circled about slowly and warily. Then with the speed of a panther Eliphal lunged at Igal, wheeled a half circle and seized him with both hands at the top and bottom of the spine. He lifted his opponent high above his head and after spinning him around, he hurled him away above the heads of the onlookers. Igal fell with a heavy thud and it was quite a while before he regained his senses.

Eliphal did not have to answer any more questions.

2.

They were a wild lot, these four hundred daredevils who held the fortified cave of Adullam, the one thing they had in common being their devotion to David. They admired and respected Eliphal, but it cannot be said that they were fond of him. He was too grave and aloof.

"He seems to be oppressed by a dark memory," said Igal who, after that tussle with Eliphal, became his fast friend.

The men noticed that it was only when David led them into a foray against the Philistines that Eliphals' face lighted up. In the encounter at Keilah he was like a famished lion, rushing in where the din and danger were greatest. The men marveled that he came out of it with only a few gashes on his arms.

But it was not often that David was able to lead his men against the foe. Those were the days when he was being hunted by King Saul, his former protector. People said that the moody king was crazed by fear and jealousy of the brilliant young leader.

For David and his followers those were days of continuous flight and alarm. Eliphal was deeply grieved.

"Why," he asked Igal, "must these two be enemies when our people are so cruelly oppressed by the Philistines?"

"I don't know," Igal replied. "But we don't ask questions. David leads and we follow. We would all lay down our lives for him, no matter where, no matter against whom."

Shortly after the battle at Keilah, Eliphal was ordered to report to the leader. The youth was scared and puzzled. Had he done anything amiss? Was he going to be punished?

"I wanted to tell you," said David, "that I know how bravely you fought at Keilah. I'd like to know more about you." He smiled and laid his hand on Eliphal's shoulder with that charm of manner which opened men's hearts to him. The gesture had a strange effect on the shy youth. He burst into tears.

The story he told resembled others that David had heard. Eliphal and his two brothers had worked at the forge and anvil with their father, who was the smith of their village. The weapons they made of bronze and iron were in great demand, but when the Philistines overran their district they commanded that no more weapons should be made in Israel.

Eliphal's father defied the command, as did other smiths in the land, for to obey it meant letting the Philistines fasten their yoke upon Israel forever. He set up a forge in a secret place in the hills, but he was betrayed. The enemy swooped down on them and slew Eliphal's father and brothers. He alone escaped, and he swore an oath that he would live on only to avenge them.

It was not easy for Eliphal to tell his story. The tears streamed down his face as he ended. When he looked up he was amazed to see that David too was weeping. A powerful emotion swept through the youth. In that moment his love for David became boundless.

3.

Not long afterwards, however, Eliphal heard strange news, so strange that he couldn't believe his ears. David was leaving Adullam to take refuge among the Philistines! There was nothing else he could do, the men said. In Judah King Saul was closing in on him. Soon he would be snared like a bird and slain.

"You are free to come with me or go your own way," said David to his men. "Let each one decide for himself."

"Where David goes, we go!" they all cried.

And to each other the men said: "David is shrewd. He will know how to dwell among the Philistines without aiding them against his people."

Eliphal, too, went with David, but his heart was heavy. What could be more cruel than to live under the protection of the enemy he hated? It was only his faith in David, and his love for him, that kept him from deserting. So he stayed on with him in the fortress of Ziklag, which the Philistines turned over to David, waiting and hoping that soon, very soon, they would return to Judah.

But one day his friend Igal brought him still stranger news.

"Eliphal," said Igal, "we are marching out of Ziklag."

"Back to Judah?" asked Eliphal eagerly.

"No," said Igal. "We are marching north along the coastal plain, then east into the Valley of Jezreel."

"But why?"

"There is going to be a big battle in the Valley. King Saul has gathered all his forces there and the Philistines are going up to meet him."

"God be praised!" cried Eliphal. "So we are going up to join the forces of Israel!"

"No," said Igal. "We are marching with the Philistines."

Eliphal stared at his friend as one would stare at a two-headed camel.

"You are out of your mind!" he finally managed to say.

"That's how it is," said Igal. "I don't know what it all means. But our protector, the King of Gath, has asked David to join his battalions, and how could David refuse? So he is going, and, naturally, we are all going with him. You may as well get ready, Eliphal, my friend," Igal concluded.

4.

They marched along the coastal plain, close to the Shephelah, Eliphal scanning the rising ground on the right, looking hard for a good place to make his break. He found it at last. He bounded into a defile, raced a short distance north, and scaling a crag, he looked down on David and his men as they filed past.

"Traitor!" he screamed. "David, you are a traitor! You and all your riff-raff!"

David glanced up for only a moment, with no change at all in his expression. But Igal, who was marching on David's right, lifted his bow from his shoulder, snatched an arrow from his quiver and was about to set it to the string. Eliphal saw David turn and strike Igal a sharp blow on the wrist. The arrow jumped out of Igal's hand and fell to the gound.

Eliphal leaped off the crag, plunged deeper into the low hills of the Shephelah, then took a northerly course towards the Valley of Jezreel. His heart was like an empty wilderness. If he could only weep, he told himself, his grief would be easier to bear. But the tears refused to come. Suddenly he remembered Igal.

"He was ready to pierce me with his arrow, me, his best friend!" he muttered. Then he remembered how David had struck the arrow from his hand.

"Why did he do it?" he moaned. "Why do I have to owe my life to this— this—." He was going to say "traitor." But for some reason the word stuck in his throat.

Eliphal reached the Valley, found the encampment of Saul's army at the foot of Mount Gilboa, and was received into one of the units. Several days later the Philistines attacked and the battle ranged over a wide area. Eliphal's weapons had their fill of the enemy, but his deeds brought him no joy. Saul's army was put to flight, three of his sons, including Jonathan, were slain, and the unhappy king ended his own life by falling on his sword.

This is all written down, and all men know it.

5.

Eliphal escaped to Beth-shan and crossed the Jordan to Jabesh-gilead. He toiled on south along the river, and when he came opposite Jericho he swam to the other side and wandered through the rocky wastes of the Negev. At a place called Maon he came upon a ragged Amalekite who told him a woeful tale of a raid which David had made upon his tribe.

"He carried off everything we had, including the booty we had taken in Ziklag," the Amalekite mourned.

"So you raided Ziklag first!" said Eliphal. "And when was that?"

"When we learned that he and his men had gone away to fight against King Saul. But he soon came back and punished us."

"So! After the Philistines, with his help, broke the strength of Israel, they let him return to Ziklag."

He raised up the youth, who was weeping in a loud voice.

"No," said the Amalekite. "He returned before the battle."

"Liar!" cried Eliphal. "David, too, fought against Israel!"

"He did not," the other said. "The Philistines sent him

away before the battle. And some say David made them
suspect him, so they should send him away. He is shrewd,
this David; and what a fighter! Shall I tell you how he
fell upon us and—"

But Eliphal had heard enough.

6.

When he came to Ziklag the sentinel who stood at the gate
of the stronghold stared at him long and hard before he
recognized him.

"Eliphal!" he cried at last. "How you have changed!
You are lean and starved like one who has not tasted food
for a month. But go inside into the court. The men are
all there. David has called an assembly."

Eliphal entered and stood on the edge of the gathering.
The men had rent their clothes in mourning, and David
was standing before them. He told them how great had
been the love between him and Jonathan. He told them
how bravely King Saul had fought and labored for his
people. And, as was his custom, he being the skilled harpist
and singer of psalms, David broke into song.

A moaning rose from the hardened men as he sang:

*Saul and Jonathan were lovely and pleasant in their
lives,*
And in their death they were not divided.

And they wept aloud when he ended with the words:

How are the mighty fallen,
And the weapons of war perished!

David was about to dismiss the assembly when Eliphal
ran forward and knelt down before him. He raised up the
ragged youth who was weeping in a loud voice.

"Eliphal!" he cried. And David put his arms around
him and embraced him and kissed him.

BEHOLD, THE TEMPLE!

In every town and village of the land the people were excited and happy. It was great news which the heralds of King Solomon had brought them. The Temple in Jerusalem was built, and ready to be dedicated.

"I, Solomon son of David, King of Israel, greet you in the name of the Lord," ran the royal decree which the heralds read to the people. "Be it known to you that by the Lord's favor, I have now completed the House which I have built Him in Jerusalem. Let every village and town, therefore, choose two men of merit and valor to go up to Jerusalem and dedicate the Lord's House with me. And when they return they will tell their people the glory which their eyes shall behold."

Now, in the town of Gizon, which lay in the fields of Gad near the border of Ammon, the first man chosen by the people was Galal, their chief elder. But whom shall they choose to go with him? They knew, of course, that no man was more worthy than Hashem. When Hashem was a young man he was one of David's famous band of heroes, the *gibborim*. The people of Gizon were still proud of his deeds against the enemies of Israel.

But Hashem was now old, very old. When he went to sit in the gateway of Gizon he was supported by his grandson Harim, a lad of thirteen. They feared that the journey to Jerusalem would be too much for his feeble frame and he would die on the way. So they chose another to accompany the chief elder to the dedication.

The two men departed and the people thought no more

about them. "Let us wait till they return," they said, "and they will tell us what they have seen and heard."

But Harim knew what bitter sorrow now lay in the heart of his grandfather. For the old man longed to go up to Jerusalem: was he not among the first of David's warriors when they captured it from the Jebusites? And he longed to see the splendor of David's son; men spoke of it with so much awe and pride. But above all, Hashem longed to see the Temple and feast his eyes upon the beauty of the House of the Lord, the God of Israel.

When the two men mounted their beasts and rode away through the gate of Gizon with the blessings of the people, Hashem's face showed no sign of his keen disappointment. There was a faraway gaze in his eyes, and his lips were set in a rigid line. But Harim knew that his heart was heavy with sorrow and longing.

It was almost a month before the two returned. The feast of dedication, as we learn from the chronicle, lasted fourteen days, and the remaining days were spent on the journey to the capital and back to Gizon. How the town rejoiced when the two arrived! A day was set apart for the people to assemble and hear their report.

The sun had only begun his downward course, but already the farmers were back from their fields and groves, and the shepherds had folded their flocks. The broad place at the gateway was thronged. Every man, woman and child, it seemed, had come to hear the report. In a place of honor near the chief elder sat old Hashem, with Harim, his grandson, standing beside him.

"My tongue," the elder began, "is too feeble to relate all the wonders I have seen. The people who came from every corner of the land were like the sands on the seashore for multitude. Our king is great and glorious. The Temple is more splendid than anything man has ever looked upon."

A sound as of a single breath rose from the listeners in the gateway. But Harim, whose arm was around his grandfather's shoulders, felt them tremble and droop.

The elder went on and spoke of the dedication. He told them how the Ark of the Covenant was brought into the Holy of Holies. He spoke of the countless sacrifices offered by the people, of the joyous music of the Levites, their singing and playing.

The elder went on to repeat the words which King Solomon spoke at the dedication. The king had prayed for the people of Israel who would come to worship in the Temple. He prayed also for all other people who might come. "For," the king had said, "they shall hear of Thy great name and Thy mighty hand, and Thy House shall be a house of prayer for all people. But," the king had gone on to say, "will God in very truth dwell on the earth? Behold, heaven and the heaven of heavens cannot contain Thee! How much less this House which I have built!"

Finally, the elder spoke about the Temple itself. He told them of its broad courts and its porch. He described the Brazen Altar that stood before the porch and the great basin which the people called the Bronze Sea. There was awe in his voice when he spoke of the two huge bronze pillars that stood at the entrance of the porch, one on each side. And he told them of the two chambers beyond the porch, the outer one which the people called the Holy Place, and the inner one, the Holy of Holies.

"I have seen the Temple when the sun rose and shed its light on it," the elder concluded. "The courts shone like the sun itself and the walls sparkled and glittered like gems. Happy the man whose eyes have beheld this splendor!"

Harim looked into his grandfather's face. He saw one teardrop after another break from his eyes and trickle down into his white beard.

It was still before dawn the following morning when the boy felt the caress of a hand on his face. He opened his eyes and his grandfather was bending over him.

"Wake up," said the old man, "and saddle the asses. We are going on a journey."

The rising sun was already flooding the world with light and joy when they were mounted and off.

"Where are we going, Grandfather?"

The boy was not in the habit of asking the old man questions, but this journey was so strange, so sudden.

"Did Isaac question his father Abraham when he led him to Mount Moriah?" the old man replied.

The boy knew the story. He knew Isaac was being taken to be sacrificed.

"I won't say a word even if you also take me to Moriah," he laughed.

"But that is the exact place to which we are going," said Hashem solemnly.

Harim pulled up his beast. He peered into his grandfather's face, and it seemed to him there was a strange look in it. A vague fear began mounting in him.

"Don't you know," the old man continued, "that the Temple stands on Mount Moriah where the angel of the Lord appeared and Isaac was saved? We are going to Jerusalem to see the Temple."

The boy took a deep breath.

"I see," he said. "But it's a long journey, isn't it?"

"Long?" said Hashem. "No journey would be too long."

"You know the way, Grandfather?"

"Have no fear. We'll get there."

They plodded on. The hot sun began to beat down on them, and the boy rejoiced to see how well the old man was bearing up. A new vigor seemed to have entered the old frame.

They turned from one path into another, moving, it seemed to the boy, in different directions. As the day wore on the sand and rocks through which they plodded looked more and more like a far-flung wilderness.

The boy suddenly halted.

"The Temple! Look, boy, it's the Temple!"

"Grandfather," he said, "we should be going west, should we not?"

"Of course," said Hashem. "We are going down to the Jordan, to the ford above Zarethan."

"But for a long time now we have been riding east.

Look, Grandfather, the sun is setting behind us," the boy
replied.

The old man halted his beast, gazed around, and seemed
to shake himself out of a trance.

"We took a wrong turn somewhere," he finally said.
"Don't let it ruffle you, boy. We'll stop here for the night
and after dawn we'll find the right path."

But neither on the morrow nor the day after could they
find the right path or, for that matter, any path. The
desert seemed endless and trackless and they were caught
in it as in a maze. There was but little shade to shelter
them from the merciless sun, and at night the boy could
hear the old man shiver with cold. On the third day their
water bottle was empty.

Hashem was now unable to sit up in the saddle. The
boy dismounted, held him up and tramped on beside him,
weeping with fear and despair. Before the day was far
advanced Hashem lay down on the sand, babbling as in
fever.

Suddenly he sat up and lifting a trembling arm, he
pointed into the distance.

"The Temple!" he cried in a voice not his own. "Look,
boy, it's the Temple!"

"Where, Grandfather, where?"

"There! Straight ahead! Do you see how the walls
flash in the sun? And the courts, the shining courts all
around! Ah, the pillars! There stand the two bronze
pillars! How tall and beautiful they are! And what is that
in front of them? Of course! It's the Brazen Altar and
near it the Bronze Sea!"

"I don't see them, Grandfather. I don't see them," the
boy wailed.

"Have you gone blind, Harim, my lad? Open your eyes
wide! It's the House of the Lord in Jerusalem! The Lord
be praised, I see it at last!"

When the two Ammonites, mounted on camels, came

upon Hashem and his grandson, they rigged up a litter between the two donkeys on which they laid the old man. Towards evening they arrived in Gizon and after receiving their reward, the Ammonites departed.

As they passed through the gate the old man tried to sit up and tell the people what he had seen. But he fell back again.

"What is he trying to say?" they asked Harim.

"He saw the Temple! Grandfather saw it!" the boy told them.

"Really?" they answered. "In the desert men have been known to see all sorts of wonders."

"It was no mirage!" Harim assured them. "He saw the same Temple as our elder saw in Jerusalem. How could it be a mirage? It was the same one, the same one!"

BROTHERS ALWAYS

Why was Shechem so crowded and excited? Why were people from every corner of the land streaming to this ancient city? The great King Solomon was no more, and his son Rehoboam had come from Jerusalem to Shechem to be crowned king in his father's place.

But what was old Mara doing in all that stir and tumult? Mara was so old she could hardly walk: she had to be helped by her granddaughter Dinah. Without Dinah she could not have made the short journey from her village near the city. Now, as she sat just inside the gate, scanning the people moving in and out, the girl stood by her side, watching her anxiously. For Mara's glance let none of the men escape her. She gazed keenly at all of them, especially the stalwart ones.

In her long life many sorrows had fallen to Mara's lot. But the saddest day of her life was when her two sons, Uriel and Shama, forsook their native village and were not heard of again.

It was now nearly ten years since they vanished, but Mara never stopped hoping that some day, even if it was her last day on earth, she would see them again. So when they told her that people from all over the land were gathering in Shechem, she said, "Uriel and Shama will also be there. I know it, I know it. I'll go to Shechem and see them before I die."

People who were told what took place in the gate of the city could hardly believe their ears. "A miracle!" they said "It was nothing else but a miracle! To think that this mother found both her lost sons on the selfsame day!"

The first one she recognized was Uriel. The old woman's heart leaped, then seemed to stop. There, in the center of the gate, amid a troop of tall blackbearded men, stood Uriel, her son Uriel!

"My son, my son!" she cried and would have fallen but for Dinah's arm which supported her.

The man ran forward swiftly and embraced his mother. And when, in their great and sudden joy, they had wept together, Uriel told her his story.

After his father's death, Uriel had grown moody and restless. In the little village he felt cramped and unhappy. So he went away secretly, for he knew he would not hold out against his mother's tears. After many wanderings he made his way to Egypt. There he met a certain Jeroboam, who had fled to Egypt to escape the wrath of King Solomon whom the man had offended. Uriel and Jeroboam became friends, and both were now back in their own country. Uriel told his mother how happy he was to be among the followers of Jeroboam, who was looked up to by the tribe of Ephraim and other tribes of Israel.

And as they stood talking, the old woman, still trembling with joy, looked up suddenly and said:

"Look, there comes Shama!"

She spoke the words calmly, as though she expected Shama to be there. The first miracle made the second one seem almost natural.

The man to whom she pointed stopped and stared, unable to believe his eyes. Then he ran forward and clasped the old woman in his arms. The two brothers embraced, and they were all so deeply moved that for a while none of them could speak.

Shama at last told his story. He had left his home to join a troop of wandering prophets. "Sons of the prophets," the people called them. They were mere youths who roamed up and down the land calling on men to be faithful to the

God of Abraham and Moses. For many years Shama led this wandering life, but now his home was in Jerusalem. He was the assistant to the chief scribe in the royal palace, and had come to Shechem to see Rehoboam crowned the new king.

The joy of finding her lost sons was nearly too much for the feeble old woman. What did it matter to her that grave events were taking place in the city? For things were not going well with Solomon's son. People were angry; they muttered and grumbled. The crowning was being put off from day to day.

All of that meant nothing to Mara. She had only one thought, one wish: to see her sons, to hear their voices, to look into their bold faces, to see their eyes grow soft when she spoke to them.

But one day she waited for them in vain.

"Dinah," she said, "What is it? What keeps them from coming today?"

"Grandmother," said Dinah, "terrible things are going on in the city. Many of the people do not want the new king. They asked him not to lay heavy burdens upon them as his father had done. And he answered: 'My father punished you with whips, but I will punish you with whips tipped with iron.' The people shouted and jeered at him. They defied him."

"Is that a reason why my sons should not come to me?" begged the old woman.

But Uriel and Shama stayed away the next day also.

"What is it, Dinah?" the old woman moaned. "Why don't they come?"

"Grandmother," said Dinah, "Today the people stoned one of the king's chief officers. The king sent him to speak to the people, but they stoned him to death."

"But my sons! Where are my sons, Dinah?" Mara repeated.

"The tribes of the north have broken away from Reho-

He ran forward and clasped the old woman in his arms.

boam, Grandmother. Their leader is Jeroboam, Uriel's friend with whom he returned from Egypt."

"Go, Dinah, find my sons and tell them to come."

"But Uriel is of those who follow Jeroboam, and Shama is of those who follow Rehoboam. Grandmother, your sons are enemies now."

"What are you saying, Dinah? My sons enemies? Go find them and bring them here. Go at once."

The girl went, but returned without them.

"Grandmother," she reported, "I saw Uriel and he said he would come only if Shama should not be here. And I saw Shama and he said he would come, but he must not find Uriel here."

The old woman looked frightened and dazed. She made her granddaughter repeat her words, but seemed unable to grasp what they meant.

"And Grandmother," Dinah continued, "the land is being torn and rent. Judah and Benjamin are going with Rehoboam, and all the other tribes are going with Jeroboam."

But the old woman was not listening.

"My sons, they are both my sons. Must I lose them again?"

Early the following morning she called Dinah to her bedside.

"Go find them," she said in a changed voice. "Tell them to come before it is too late."

The girl ran, but it was hours before she found them and delivered her message to them.

The first to arrive was Uriel. But he was already too late. He could only close his mothers unseeing eyes. Shortly afterwards came Shama. He knelt by the bed-side and sobbed bitterly. Opposite him stood his brother, the tears streaming down his face.

Shama rose to his feet. The two men looked into each other's eyes. Then, with one accord, they clasped hands across the bed.

"We are still brothers," said Uriel.

"Brothers always," Shama answered.

ABIEL AND THE PROPHET

Bedan, who lived in Ataroth in the Kingdom of Israel, was a wise man. That, at any rate, was the opinion of his fellow-townsmen, and other people, too, were of the same opinion. They often came to Bedan for advice in matters that vexed and baffled them.

"I will go to Ataroth and seek out this wise man and he will tell me what to do with Abiel," said Shallum, a farmer of Beeroth, to Adah his wife. "Myself, I can do nothing with this son of ours."

"Abiel is only a lad," said Adah, "and he will be a good man, with the Lord's help. But if you think Bedan, too, can help, go and the Lord prosper your journey."

So Shallum went to Ataroth with a lamb and a piece of silver for Bedan, and told him his story.

"My son Abiel will soon be sixteen years old. He is a sturdy lad with some skill to fashion implements of wood and metal, and he makes sweet sounds with the pipe and other instruments of music. But I cannot bend his will to the labor of the field or grove or pasture. On the field he spends more time daydreaming than plowing or hoeing. In the pasture his sheep stray off while he sits blowing his pipe, and the sound of his pipe is always sad. In the town he doesn't mingle with the other lads, but sits apart, moody and listless. Other lads have eyes for the maids who come to draw water at the well, but not he. And to all my warnings and rebukes he has only one answer: 'I have no joy in the things around me. They are vain, and to no purpose.' And I ask him: Why do you sit aloof from others, listening to the silence? 'I listen for an answer to my longing,' he says. Nor can I make him say more, though his meaning is beyond my understanding."

Thus spoke Shallum, the farmer of Beeroth, to Bedan, the wise man of Ataroth. Bedan sat a long time without saying a word. He sat and pondered. Finally he spoke.

"Your son," he said, "feels cramped in his native village. Every day it's the same fields and houses, the same hills and groves, the same people. Send him out where he will see new sights, where people gather from all over the land. He will see palaces instead of huts, and the lords of the land instead of poor and lowly husbandmen. He will come back with new spirit and pride, for people will listen to him with wonder. The place is not too far. It is Bethel, the shrine city of the Kingdom of Israel. Let him stay there a few days and take along a bullock for a sacrifice on the altar."

When Shallum returned he said to Adah, his wife:

"The wise man told me to send Abiel to Bethel. It will lift up his heart, he said."

"Then let him go," said Adah. "But this I know: when a camel goes to Jerusalem and comes back, he is still a camel."

His father gave Abiel the finest bullock of his herd, and off went the lad to Bethel, where the rich and the noble of the Kingdom of Israel came with droves of cattle for the altar of the shrine. In return, they would win the favor of God and prosper in all their ways. So, at any rate, they believed.

In three days, Abiel returned to his native village, and when his father peered into his face, his heart sank. In Abiel's eyes he saw more sadness than before. The lad was even more moody and restless. What did it mean? He had done as the wise man said, but his son was not cured.

Shallum plied the lad with questions. Had he seen the shrine and the priests, great and small? Had he seen the high priest, Amaziah? Had he seen the palaces and gardens, the street and the market place, the lords and the princes? Abiel just nodded his head by way of answer, but after several days he opened his heart to his father and told him what it was that made his spirit droop so low.

"It's because of the prophet. I listened to his words and I can't forget them."

"What prophet?" his father asked.

"He called himself Amos and he came from the village of Tekoa in the Kingdom of Judah."

"A prophet from Judah, and his words smote your heart? What, then, did he say?"

"He was bold and fearless, this prophet," Abiel answered. "He told the grand lords and ladies that God spurns their sacrifices. He told the rich they were oppressing the poor and crushing the needy."

Father and son were silent awhile

"It is true, father, isn't it?" Abiel finally asked.

"Alas, it is," the man sighed. "I have seen poor farmers sell themselves as slaves to pay their debts."

"They buy the poor for silver and the needy for a pair of shoes. Those were the words of the prophet from Judah," said Abiel.

"But, my son, why do you let it make you unhappy? Can we change all that?" the man pleaded.

"Amos of Tekoa told them what they must do," the lad replied. "Let justice well up as waters, he cried, and righteousness as a mighty stream."

"Wonderful words, my son, but how can we make men take them to heart?"

"Our people must live by them, he said. If they don't, they are not true to their God, and He will punish them."

"I can see that he is a brave and good man, your prophet," said Shallum sadly. "But you, Abiel, what will become of you? He has robbed you of the joy of life."

"And something else, father," the lad hastened to add. "This Amaziah, the high priest of Bethel, ordered Amos to leave the Kingdom of Israel. 'Go into the land of Judah, and prophesy there,' he commanded him. That was a great wrong, wasn't it?"

"And will you take it upon yourself to right every wrong that men do?" said Shallum.

"I can at least let him know that I stand by his side," the lad replied.

"What do these words mean?" Shallum demanded. But Abiel would say no more.

Again Shallum went to see the man of Ataroth whom men called wise. His wife saw him depart and only said: "May the second seedling grow better than the first."

Shallum brought the man two lambs and two pieces of silver, and told him all that befell his son in Bethel.

"And now," Shallum ended, "I fear greatly that the lad has it in his heart to go away and that he will go to Judah to the prophet Amos and stay with him."

"You must on no account let him go!" the wise man declared. "This Amos has already done him great harm, and if he goes' and lives with him, he will ruin the poor boy altogether."

Shallum hurried back to Beeroth as fast as he could, but when he arrived it was too late. Abiel was gone.

But Shallum's wife spoke to him and said:

"Do not go looking for him. If it is God's will that he should return, he will do so without urging on your part. If not, all your pleas and commands will only harden his resolve. He has no doubt gone to seek the prophet of Judah. Heaven grant that he may show our son the right path to follow. As for the wise man of Ataroth, save your lambs and your pieces of silver. I know my son well, and I say the wise man's wisdom is too short to reach out to him."

Shallum heard his wife with surprise. Never before had she spoken to him so long and with so much assurance. Her words lodged in his heart and he did as she said.

Nevertheless, as one week passed and a second and then

"Master, I have found you, I have found you at last!"

a third, he became anxious and restless. His wife observed him closely and she said to him: "Wait one more week, and after that you will go and look for him and see if he is well."

But before the fourth week was over Abiel came back

to his father's house. The news spread quickly in the village and the people rejoiced. But Shallum, of course, was most joyful of all. For not only did he have his son again, but the first glance revealed to him that a great and happy change had come over the lad.

When the sun went down and the neighbors who had come to bid him welcome home had departed, Abiel told his father and mother the things that had befallen him.

"I wandered for nearly a week through towns and villages," he related, "across vales and over many heights. I came at last to the village of Tekoa in the Kingdom of Judah. I said to the people: Tell me where I will find the prophet Amos. I have come a long distance from the Kingdom of Israel to seek him out. The people looked at me with wonder and said: The prophet Amos? There is no one in Tekoa who is called the prophet Amos. There is one called Amos who is a herdsman and a dresser of sycamore trees, and he is the only Amos in our village. I marveled greatly, but I said: Take me to him. And when I stood before him, it was he, the prophet who prophesied in Bethel! He was tending his sheep in a pasture not far from the village. I stooped to the ground at his feet.

"Master, I cried, the Lord be praised! I have found you, I have found you at last!

"He lifted me up and embraced me, and I told him who I was, and who my father was, and why I had come to him. Day and night I had no rest, I told him, because of the longing with which the words he spoke at Bethel had filled my heart.

"He looked keenly at me and said nothing. But I felt his eyes pierce through me like arrows. At last he spoke. Bide with me two weeks, he said, and after that you will know what you must do.

"So I stayed with him and rose up in the early dawn and took the sheep to pasture. He sent me off with a blessing that cheered my heart, and when I blew my pipe the song that flowed from it was happy and joyous. I labored with him in his grove and together we sorted the sycamore figs and packed them for the market.

"At night we folded the sheep and ate our barley cakes, giving thanks to the Lord for his bounty, and spoke only of the day's labor and of the tasks that must be done on the morrow. The words he spoke were simple, but they lighted up my heart like the sun when it shines down into a dark valley.

"So the two weeks ended and he said to me: Now you know what you must do. And I said: Yes, I must go back to my father's fields and flocks and do my daily tasks. He blessed me and kissed me and said: Go in peace. Some day you too may lift up your voice and prophesy. But wait. Wait till the spirit of the Lord moves you as it moved upon the face of the water on the Day of Creation. For when the Lord has spoken, who can but prophesy?"

The lad fell silent and Shallum and his wife were also silent. At length the woman said:

"This is the heart of wisdom. It is not only in words that are spoken, but in words that are left unspoken. It is in simple deeds that are done, and in the light that flows from the eyes and enters another's heart."

And when she said this Shallum marveled and said to himself: "Lo! it is she, my wife, who is wise! And all these years I have not known it!"

THE AVENGER

Ozam was worried. Eliel, his son, was acting strangely. Ozam went to his friend, the prophet Isaiah, for advice.

"I fear my son will do something rash," he said. "Ever since he heard that Assyrian scoff at the God of Israel he hasn't been the same. 'He must not go unpunished,' he keeps on repeating, and I fear he plans to do the punishing himself."

"I know your son," the prophet replied. "He is a gentle lad, and not prone to bloodshed."

"Yes, but he can't forget how Rabshakeh stood near the wall of Jerusalem, mocking and defying the Holy One of Israel. I was there, too, when he cried to the archers on the wall: 'Why do you listen to your King Hezekiah? Don't you know that my master, King Sennacherib, has placed his yoke on the necks of many lands and nations? Were the gods of those lands able to deliver them? Why, then, do you think that your God will be able to deliver Jerusalem?' And by the side of this scoffer stood the commander of the Assyrian host, the man they call the Tartan."

"All this, my friend, was reported to me by the king," said Isaiah, laying his hand on Ozams' shoulder to calm him, "and you know what reply I told the king to send to Rabshakeh and his master Sennacherib."

"Of course I know, and all Jerusalem knows. You told him to say that Zion despises him and laughs him to scorn. And you promised our people that Sennacherib will not come into our city or even shoot an arrow into it."

"And you have no more faith in my words, old friend?" the prophet spoke sadly.

"I? Of course, I have!" Ozam declared. "But this proud, hot-blooded son of mine! This is what he said to me yesterday: 'It is many days now since the prophet spoke those words. But see what has been going forward all this time. The Assyrian hosts are established opposite Jerusalem. They are raising their mounds and setting up their engines. Soon they will blockade the city entirely, cutting off our food and water. And their engines will batter our walls, and hurl stones into the heart of the city."

"Nevertheless, the word I spoke to the king stands," said Isaiah.

"But Eliel is like a wild colt. 'The scoffer will go unpunished,' he keeps on saying."

"Then I have a word for your son," said the prophet. "Let a man defend his own right and honor, but the Holy One of Israel will choose his own instrument to avenge Him."

2.

The word of the prophet had a soothing effect on the youth, but the calm lasted only a few days. The storm within him broke out again with even greater force. He saw the mounds before the city rise higher. He saw the battering rams and other siege engines multiply. He saw the ring around the city grow tighter.

On a night when he was standing sentry on a battlement facing the Kidron Valley, Eliel fastened the end of a long rope around an upright of the parapet, and let himself down to the foot of the wall. It was a moonless night; the stars flickered feebly through the driving clouds.

His aim was clear enough in his mind: to plunge his dagger through the heart of the man who had mocked the God of Israel. But how he would carry out this desperate aim was anything but clear to him. He must make the attempt, let it succeed or fail.

Slowly and noiselessly he crawled among the rocks and growths that strewed the valley. At length the slope of the Mount of Olives loomed before him.

"Strange, there is no sentinel at the base of the Mount," he said to himself. With even greater caution he pulled himself up the slope and the outlines of the Assyrian encampment stood out against the blackness. Still no sentinel.

Eliel's wonder grew, but as he continued to climb towards the summit he heard the sound of voices and the thud of wooden and metal objects throughout the camp. The entire host seemed to be astir. As Eliel came closer he could make out swarms of shadows moving swiftly about. Tents were coming down and huge implements were being dragged away, clattering along the bumpy ground.

The Assyrian host was an army of hurrying shadows, a dream army, sprung from the bowels of the earth. Only the muffled commands that broke through the darkness and the rumble across the mount gave Eliel the assurance that he was not asleep and dreaming.

The truth flashed in upon him like a blinding light.

"They are breaking camp! The enemy is breaking camp!" he cried out as he stood up. That was why there were no sentinels! That was why no torches lighted up the scene. The flare of torches would give the secret away to the people of Jerusalem.

Eliel stood up, looked around a few moments, then walked boldly into the camp and mingled with the shadows. No one paid any attention to him. Why are they doing this? he kept wondering. But to seek an answer from the enemy would have been too dangerous.

He wandered about amid the debris, in the midst of which hardly a tent was still standing. But off towards the east, on the outer fringe of the encampment, he spied one that still stood erect. As he came closer he saw a soft green light shine faintly through a large opening in it. It was the opening of the entrance flap, and through it came the sound of voices. Eliel lay down on the ground and listened.

He could tell it was the Aramaic language in which two voices were speaking. He knew the language well. But the voices were so low, he was unable to make out the words. With startling suddenness, however, they became loud and harsh.

"Tirhakah, Tirhakah!" one of the voices rasped. "I am tired of hearing that name! Who is this Tirhakah? Some pigmy prince from Ethiopia, coming up with a horde of savages, whom one or two battalions of Assyrians should be enough to scatter to the winds! And because of this Tirhakah, we, the flower of Sennacherib's might, must pull down everything we have built up for the capture of this city, and decamp! What has become of the other cohorts of the king? Have they all been stricken dead?"

"That's enough, Tartan!" the other voice snapped back. "You are forgetting your place! Are you perhaps conducting the affairs of the Assyrian empire? I am here to bring you the king's orders, and you are here to carry them out!"

"Your tongue is as sharp as ever, Rabshakeh, my friend," the Tartan sneered. "But it's you who are forgetting your place. Do you think you are now speaking to some frightened or defeated chieftain?"

At the sound of that name Eliel started up and his hand reached for the hilt of his long dagger. But he held back. Rabshakeh's reply came in a voice choked with rage.

"I am the king's messenger, and when I stand before you it's the same as if the king himself stood before you!" he snarled.

"No, Rabshakeh, it is not the same," the Tartan came back. "I'll tell you how I feel when you stand before me. I feel sick when I look at you! And something else I'll tell you. Do you know the real cause of this evil that has come upon us. It's you, Rabshakeh, you!"

"Is there no limit to your insolence?" Rabshakeh roared.

"Do you remember when we two stood before the city?" the Tartan went on calmly, his voice cold and hard. "You taunted those people and their king. You sneered at them. And you mocked at their God, and flouted Him. Could the other gods save their people from the hands of my king? you jeered. Why, then, do you think your God can save you? And when I heard you, Rabshakeh, I knew in my heart that your words would bring us doom!"

"You are a fool, Tartan, an impudent fool!" the other bellowed.

"I am a plain and blunt soldier," the Tartan replied. "I worship my own gods, but I respect the gods that other people worship. Besides, the God of these people is different from others. Wise men have told me about Him. He rules the heavens and the earth, and he cannot be seen or shaped in an image of wood or stone. He is more fearful and more powerful than the others. And you, Rabshakeh, stirred up His wrath with that proud and stupid tongue of yours."

"Rein in your tongue, Tartan, or—" Rabshakeh shouted.

"Softly, my brave minister!" the Tartan warned. "Let your sword sleep in its sheath if you don't want to feel the edge of mine!"

"Draw it, then, and we'll see which has the sharper edge!" Rabshakeh cried.

Eliel heard the clash and clang of the swords, but the ringing sounds ended quickly. A deep groan swept through the open flap of the tent, followed by a heavy thud. A shadow stooped through the opening and stalked away, straight and tall, into the darkness.

Eliel had no doubt as to who the tall figure was. He had seen it before standing beside Rabshakeh before the wall of Jerusalem.

When Eliel got back to the city the Assyrian retreat was already known. The streets were thronged with people. The city rang with their joyous cries.

"Eliel," said Ozam to his son, "the Lord has heard our

The tall figure stalked away into the darkness

prayer. Isaiah's prophecy has come true."

"And He has chosen His own instrument to avenge Him upon His enemy," the youth added.

He said no more at the moment. He felt a need to be alone and to ponder on what he saw and heard that night in the ghostly camp of the Assyrians.

THE TROWEL AND THE SWORD

There, now," said the old man to the trowel and sword, "I've given you a good scrubbing and you look bright and happy, both of you."

"Now," he continued, "I'll put you up where you belong. You know where that is, don't you? You've been hanging there for nearly fifty years." And he hung them on the wall of his chamber where they gleamed and glittered as they caught the rays that filtered in through the lattice. Then he sat down on a mat against the opposite wall, and the yellowed skin of his face glowed as he looked at them.

"Not so hard to make you look fresh and young," he went on with a chuckle. "But me! Oh, well, I feel young again when I look at you and remember those days—those days—" And the white beard began to droop down towards his chest.

"I'm dozing again," he roused himself. "Strange the way I get drowsy after polishing these two— these two—"

"There!" said the trowel to the sword. "He is asleep again, the old master."

"As usual," said the sword to the trowel. "I don't know why he has to scrub us so often. I don't mind a little rust, do you?" A light breeze came rustling in through the lattice, making the old sword rattle.

"Stop that!" said the trowel. "Do you have to rattle still —at your age? You'll wake up the master!"

"Sorry," said the sword. "An old habit. Hard to shake off. Besides I—" the sword stopped, too shy to go on.

"Say it, old blade, say it!" the trowel urged him on.

"Well, if you want the truth, I feel better when I rattle

a little. You see, hanging on a wall so many years, well—it's no life for a sword."

"It's no life for a trowel, either," the other sighed.

"It's not like the good old days, hey?" said the sword.

"Ah, the good old days," the trowel sighed again.

"When the master always had me on his side when he worked—and even when he slept," the sword boasted.

"And me?" the trowel demanded. "I hope you won't deny that I had something to do with rebuilding the broken-down wall around Jerusalem."

"Without me the wall would never have been rebuilt," said the sword with a clang. "Do you remember how the enemies tried to stop the work?"

"Look here, old blade," the trowel complained, "you don't have to claim all the credit, do you?"

But the sword was in no mood to listen. The memories of the past came rushing in on him like a flood.

"There was that day when the master led a troop of builders through a breach of the wall against the enemy. You, my friend, were not there, for as soon as the trumpet sounded the warning, he dropped you in his basket of mortar. Me he unbuckled from his girdle and was off. We came to a place where the wall was broken down, and there was the enemy in the valley below, scurrying up the slope like a pack of wolves."

"And Nehemiah?" asked the trowel. "Where was Nehemiah?" The trowel had now forgotten that he was peeved.

"Nehemiah was right there with us! Where else would a leader like Nehemiah be? He was mustering the bow-men and spearmen. But the enemy came in such numbers our arrows seemed to make no difference. Then the word passed among us that Sanballat himself was leading them!"

"Ah, the crafty Samaritan!" the trowel grated.

"Yes, and Tobiah the Ammonite, and Geshem the Arabian," the sword clanged on. "They had made up their mind to put an end to the rebuilding of the wall that very day. And do you know why they failed? Because we didn't wait for them to get to us. We rushed out to meet them. And the man in the lead was our master."

"Our master!" the trowel echoed in a tinkling whisper.

"What blows he dealt with me that day!" the sword rattled on. "I've been in many a scrimmage in my life, but that one was just about the hottest of all. Do you see this notch in my edge? I got it that day from the blade of a giant Ammonite."

"You did? You did?" the trowel jingled with excitement. "And what happened to him, the Ammonite?"

"You have to ask?" the sword glinted with pride. "He never swung his blade again. And what praise the master received that day from Nehemiah! It was a great day for me, the greatest in my life."

"Shall I tell you what the happiest day in my life was?" The trowel tinkled softly after a long pause. "It was the day the new wall was dedicated. Of course, you remember it, old pal. How could anyone who was there ever forget it? I still hear the trumpets of the priests and the singing of the Levites. And what a shout went up when the two processions met! You remember the two processions? One was led by Nehemiah, the other by Ezra, and they met at the Gate of the Guard near the temple. But I remember best what the master said to me when it was all over."

"He said something to me, too," the sword put in.

"'Old trowel,'" he said to me, 'your handle is warped, your edges are chipped, your surface is battered, but I love you. You and I—we helped build the wall of Jerusalem. We made the city safe to live in.'"

"He said that to you?" the sword rang softly. "The same words, almost, he said to me. 'With one hand we built, with the other we held the sword,' he said to me. 'Without you the city would still have no wall.'"

"So he polished both of us until we shone, and hung us

"The man in the lead was our master!"

up side by side," the trowel added.

"That was a long time ago," the sword clinked softly.

"A long, long time ago," the trowel whispered.

There was another pause and the sword said:

"Look, he's beginning to stir."

"He's had a good long nap," said the trowel.

"His face is shining as if someone polished it," said the sword.

"And do you see the way he smiles?" said the trowel. "It's a smile of remembrance. He, too, remembers."

OHAD'S SHARE

Ohad the scout stood before his captain, head bowed and silent.

"Speak," said the captain.

"I hear trumpets and cymbals, Captain. I hear the Levites singing and I see flaming torches in the court of the Temple," said the scout.

"Of course, you do," said the captain. "This is the first night of the dedication. The Temple has been cleansed, the idols of the Greeks have been swept out, the God of Israel is again being worshiped in His Temple."

"I am a Levite, Captain. I used to sing in the Temple." Ohads' voice trembled.

The captain looked keenly at the soldier.

"I know how you feel," he said. "You would like to be there, singing with the others."

"For this I fought, Captain. For this I prayed. Three times I was wounded. But I gave my blood willingly, hoping I would see this day."

"So you see it, my man, and thank the Lord for it."

"But I am not present at the dedication, Captain. I am having no share in it."

Tears broke from the man's eyes and became lost in his black beard.

For a while the captain looked at Ohad in silence.

"Why have you come to me?" he said at last.

"Captain," the man begged, "give me permission to go to the Temple so I can join the Levites—only for to-night, the first night."

Again the captain looked hard at his man.

"Ohad," he said, "you are one of my best scouts. And you know why our battalion has been stationed here, don't you?"

"Yes, Captain, but I—have I not earned the right to share—to have a share in the dedication?"

"We are here," the captain went on sternly, not heeding the man's words, "to prevent the enemy in the Akra from breaking out and raiding other sections of the city. We have driven the Syrians out of Jerusalem, but this fortress, this stronghold, is still in their hands. Look at it, Ohad, looming there in the darkness like a black shadow. We have them cooped up there, but the Akra is too strong for us to storm. So we must keep them cooped up in it. You know all that, don't you?"

"Yes, Captain. But can't you spare me one night—just to-night?"

"No, Ohad! No one can be singled out for special favors. Not at a time when we must all be on guard. Go back to your post, Ohad!"

Ohad left the camp of the battalion and strode on towards the Akra. He felt heart-sore, bitter and reckless. Instead of crouching, as he always did when moving towards enemy ground, he walked straight and erect.

He became aware that he was now closer to the fortress than he had ever been before, and he knelt down behind a rock to peer and listen. The winter sky was overcast. Only rarely did a gleam of starlight break through the driving clouds.

For a long time the only sounds he heard came from the faraway Temple area where the dedication rites were still in progress. Now the sounds were faint and fitful. Was it singing that he heard? He was not sure. Now and then the blast of a trumpet, thin but clear, fell upon his ears.

All at once his attention shifted. He shut his ears to whatever sounds came from behind him, from the Temple area, from the camp of his battalion lying between the Temple and the Akra. His ears became focused on sounds that came from the Akra itself. They were faint, stealthy sounds.

He left his sheltering rock and crawled closer to the fortress. He was so close now he was sure he saw the glint of the iron bars on the huge frontal gate. The gate was closed, nevertheless the sounds were now clearer. Where did they come from?

Suddenly he knew the answer. They came from two side gates, one on each flank of the fortress. Those gates were open, and from each of them one shadow after another came flitting out into the night like bats from a garret. They did not meet and melt together, these flocks of shadows. On the contrary, they moved off in opposite directions.

In a flash Ohad knew what it all meant. The enemy was sending out two columns to surround the Judean battalion and crush it in a pincers movement. They would surprise and rout the Judeans, and the way to the Temple area would be open to them. They would break in upon the feast of dedication, throw the people into panic, and scatter them. Before Judah could muster enough troops to repel them, they would be safe again behind the walls of their fortress.

Ohad turned and sped back to the camp with the swiftness of a hart.

The captain listened to him and spoke a few brief commands almost in a whisper.

"There is to be no blowing of horns and no shouting," he ordered his lieutenants. "We will surprise those who are coming to surprise us. You, Ohad, come with me and stay by my side."

Two silent lines moved out from each flank of the encampment. Lying on the ground or crouching behind rocks, the men held their weapons and waited. From the Temple

"Your share, Ohad, was greater than mine!"

area snatches of music were blown in by the gusty wind.

From each side a flock of hurrying shadows drew closer. They halted and moved forward again. A whisper passed along the Judean ranks. Several hundred bow-thongs twanged together The shadows wavered and stopped. But before they could break and run, the two Judean lines moved out and closed around them. Very few of them reached the shelter of the Akra's walls.

"Shall we report the action to the Supreme Commander, Captain," asked one of the lieutenants.

"No," said the captain. "It will be time enough tomorrow. Tonight Judah and the people are rededicating the Temple. Tonight war and battles should be far from their thoughts."

The following morning Ohad was ordered to report to the captain.

"Ohad," said the officer, "you will come with me to headquarters."

"I, Captain?" Ohad stammered. "I— why should I—"

"You will do as you are ordered," the captain cut him short.

They stood before Judah the Maccabee and the captain reported what took place the previous night before the Akra.

"And this," he ended his report, "is Ohad, the scout who got close enough to the enemy to discover his plan."

Judah laid his hand on Ohad's shoulder, and a thrill passed through the scout's frame.

"He is a Levite, General," the captain went on. "He used to sing in the Temple. Last night he was heartbroken because he could have no share in the dedication."

"No share?" Judah exclaimed. "Your share, Ohad, was greater than mine! It was greater than the share of anyone I can think of."

And the Commander looked into Ohad's eyes with that smile on his lips and gleam in his eyes that drew the hearts of men towards him like a magnet.

THE SECRET WEAPON

1

The sun had already darted its first ray over the horizon when Elazar and Shimon came upon a nomad encampment not far from Beersheba. The sight of the black tents and of people moving about among them made them keenly aware how tired and hungry they were.

"Looks like a good place to rest and refresh ourselves," said Elazar.

"And the risk?" Shimon asked.

"No chance of Romans in this place," Elazar replied. "They consider the nomads harmless."

"But how will we get food from these people? We have nothing to pay for it."

"I have," said Elazar with a grin, scooping up a handful of silver coins from a pocket inside his tunic.

"Where in the world did you get them?" Shimon marveled.

"From the centurion whom I gave that tight hug," Elazar explained. "I had an idea we would need them and it was plain that he would not."

"Elazar," said Shimon, "I am a lucky man. Where would I now be without you? And to think," he added, "that in the Roman arena I might have killed you!"

"Or the other way around," said Elazar.

The gray and wrinkled nomad whom they asked for food and water stared at them gloomily. But he dared not order them away. The two young giants before him looked too dangerous. When, however, Elazar extended his huge palm and the nomad saw two shining coins in it his eyes bulged and glittered. Bowing low, he said:

"I bid you welcome to my tent. What is a little coin more or less between loyal friends? All that we have is yours."

Elazar gave the old rogue an extra coin, and he and Shimon ate and drank their fill. They also obtained two leather scrips and two gourds in which they stored food and water before resuming their journey.

2.

It was a flight rather than a journey on which the two were embarked. They were fleeing from the Romans, nor could they be sure that whatever road they took would not lead them into the arms of the enemy. For the Roman legions, having captured Jerusalem and burnt down the Temple, were now combing the land to stamp out any sparks of rebellion that might still be smoldering.

The two youths, therefore, hid by day and walked stealthily by night. They hoped it might be their good fortune to find one of the Zealot bands which they knew were still harassing the enemy from their lairs in the deserts and jungles.

One piece of good fortune had already been granted them. The two had succeeded in escaping from a fate which they considered worse than death at the hands of the enemy.

Together with a number of other youthful captives they were being conducted by a Roman guard along the seacoast towards Egypt. They knew what lay in store for them. In Alexandria they would be put on board a ship that would take them to Rome. In the imperial capital they would, after a brief period of training, be enrolled as gladiators.

For that was the practice of the Roman conqueror. He selected the tallest and strongest youths of the lands he conquered and compelled them to fight with deadly weapons in the arena. They fought each other or they were pitted against wild and famished beasts. A huge throng of Romans watched with delight as the youths slew each other or were torn by the beasts. Such was the amusement that was dear to the hearts of the Roman rabble and nobility, including the emperor himself.

It was the strength and courage of Elazar that saved this particular group from that fate. After a long and grueling march the Romans and their prisoners had halted for the night not far from the Brook of Egypt. Each captive's wrists were tied together with strong leather thongs, and to make doubly sure the centurion in command posted a sentry to stand guard over them.

Shortly after midnight the centurion appeared and found the sentry seated on a rock, slumped over and fast asleep. The Roman officer acted swiftly and in true Roman fashion. He drew his short-sword and brought its edge down hard on the neck of the sleeping sentry. But before he could sheathe his weapon Elazar, who was lying awake just behind him, sprang to his feet and passing the circle of his arms over the Roman's head, pressed his bound wrists like a vise against his throat.

Elazar's movement was so deft and swift that his victim was unable to utter a sound. When the Roman lay limp and lifeless on the ground Elazar wrenched the sword from his grip and woke up his nearest neighbor, who happened to be Shimon. With sword tight in Elazar's grip, Shimon cut his own thongs through against its edge, and then cut the thongs that bound Elazar's wrists. The two then did the same for the other prisoners.

Silently the group sped eastward. After covering a safe distance from the sleeping Romans, they halted and decided it would be best for them to scatter and go off in pairs in different directions.

"There are bands of Zealots still fighting the Romans.

Seek them out and join them," Elazar told them. And he added:

"We don't know what awaits us. But this, at least, we have accomplished: we will not have to slay each man his brother for the pleasure of the enemy."

3.

Elazar and Shimon rested in the nomad camp and when night fell they continued their rugged journey north and east through the rocky wastes of the Negev. They moved warily and slowly. After weeks of toil and peril they reached the Jordan Valley. They plunged into the jungles north of Jericho and came at last upon a band of Zealot guerrillas, who welcomed them.

In the months that followed the band surprised and cut down a number of enemy patrols who were scouring the region. Shimon and Elazar were in the forefront of these actions. Their comrades were proud of them. They also found nicknames for them. They called the first "Swift-as-a-Deer," and the second "Strong-as-a-Lion."

But the enemy sent more and bigger patrols into the valley. The band was surprised in its turn and those that escaped scattered in every direction.

Elazar and Shimon turned south again. They had heard that near the southern end of the Dead Sea the fortress of Masada was holding out against a large Roman force that was besieging it.

"We'll try to steal into the fortress," said Elazar. "Sooner or later, I suppose, the enemy will take it. But the place is strong and he can be made to pay a high price for it."

"Making the enemy pay dearly is all we can hope for," Shimon agreed.

The first feeble light of a dawn was paling the eastern sky when, having mounted a tall cliff, they looked ahead, and made out the walls and turrets of a fortress perched

He pressed his bound wrists like a vise against the Roman's throat

on a height in the gray distance.

"Masada!" Elazar whispered. "We'll find a hiding place for the day, and this night or the next will, I hope, find us behind those walls."

Not far from the foot of the cliff they found the entrance

to a cave and stepped inside. A shadow rose up from the
ground and faced them. In the light that now flowed in
through the entrance they saw an old man, small, thin and
shaggy, staring at them through bushy eyebrows.

"Welcome to my dwelling!" he called out in their own
tongue. "And whither are you bound in this desolate
region?"

"We are on the way to Masada," Elazar explained.

"Why to Masada?" the old man asked.

"To help defend it against the Romans," Shimon replied.

"You are too late," the old man told them. "The Romans
entered Masada two weeks ago."

The two young warriors looked at each other mournfully.

"Our last fortress," said Shimon almost in a whisper.

"Our last, did you say?" the old man queried, and there
was a curious note in his voice. "I am an old man," he
went on after a pause. "But if I were young and strong I
know what I would do."

"What?" they asked.

"I would go to Yavneh," he announced slowly. Then in
a loud voice he turned to them and cried: "Go there, young
men! Go to Yavneh!"

"Yavneh?" Elazar wondered. "We skirted the place when
the Romans marched us down the coast on the way to Egypt.
It's a ramshackle town, impossible to defend. Why should
we go there?"

"Go to Yavneh," the old man repeated, "and ask for
Johanan ben Zakkai. He is forging a secret weapon against
the enemy. Ask no questions and go!" he concluded with a
ring of command in his voice.

4.

"Why are we going?" said Shimon to Elazar as they
entered Beersheba a few weeks later. He had asked the
question many times before, and always Elazar replied:

"Why not? It may as well be Yavneh as any other place."

"I am wondering, Elazar, if the old hermit in the cave was in his right mind," Shimon continued this time. "What did he mean by the secret weapon? And Yavneh, he told us before we left, is our new fortress. Fortress, indeed! One good-sized Roman patrol could easily—"

"Shimon," Elazar broke in. "Let us stop wondering. We are going to Yavneh."

They arrived at last, and after several days they were ushered into the presence of the man whose name was on the lips of everyone in the town. They stood before the famous teacher and sage Johanan ben Zakkai. A small group of his disciples stood beside him.

The two rugged warriors felt timid and nervous. But the first words and, even more, the expression of the sage put them at ease. It was gentle as well as commanding.

At his request they gave him a full account of what had befallen them since the capture of Jerusalem. He was eager for every detail and was especially interested in their adventures with the Zealot band in the Jordan Valley.

When they were done and had answered all his questions he was silent awhile. Then he spoke, slowly and gravely.

"In this place," he said, "we continue the struggle against the enemy. Not, however, with weapons of iron, of which the enemy has more than we. Here our weapons are of the spirit. Our sword is faith and learning. Our shield is worship and good deeds. The enemy has no weapons to match them. He doesn't even know they exist. With this sword and this shield our people will conquer and go on living."

A new light shone in the faces of the youthful warriors as they listened. They understood enough of what he said to feel the surge of a new hope uplift their hearts.

Johanan asked them to come closer and took a hand of each one into his own hands.

"So you, Shimon, they called Swift-as-a-Deer, and you,

Elazar, they called Strong-as-a-Lion," he said, smiling on them.

"Yes, master," they replied.

At this point one of the disciples stepped forward.

"Master," he said eagerly, "may I offer a motto and precept as a guide to them and all of us?"

"Speak," said the sage.

"Be swift as a deer and strong as a lion to do the will of your Father Who is in Heaven," said the disciple. And Johanan ben Zakkai nodded his approval.

THE CHOICE

Two fishermen off the coast of Egypt near Alexandria pulled in their net one day and found in it a silver tube, sealed at both ends. After much labor they opened it and drew out a parchment scroll covered with writing. They took the scroll to a learned Moslem, a mullah, who declared the writing to be in the Hebrew tongue, and he in turn took it to a Jewish sage who dwelt in the city. And this is the story which the sage found on the scroll.

Who will deny that the journey from Cordova to Itil, which Isaac ben Eliezer and I, Nathan ben Ezra, accomplished, was the longest and most daring that any man ever undertook? Think of the vast distance from Cordova in Spain to Itil, the capital of Khazaria, which lies at the mouth of the Volga River. What a multitude of lands we crossed! What rude and savage people we came upon! What strange rites and customs we witnessed! What perils we overcame!

I am now on my way back to Cordova, Isaac ben Eliezer having left Itil two months ago without me. He could wait no longer, he told me. He must hasten back and report to his master, Hasdai ibn Shaprut, who sent us on our strange mission.

This mission, Isaac felt, had been accomplished. He had delivered Hasdai's letter to King Joseph, the ruler of Khazaria, and was taking back to Hasdai the king's reply. He knew, of course, what the king said in his reply, and so did I. Isaac ben Eliezer was satisfied, but I was not.

"Isaac," I said to him, "the king does not really answer the most important one of Hasdai's questions. Why, I cannot say. It may be because he doesn't know or because he thinks it wiser not to answer it. But I am about to learn the truth of the matter, so I will stay on until I do. Return, therefore, without me and heaven prosper your journey. You are taking the land route by which we came. I will take the sea route, and if the winds and waves are kind, we may arrive in Cordova at the same time."

My ship is now crossing the Black Sea on the way to the Golden Horn and the Mediterranean. But the winds and waves have been anything but kind. I am haunted by the fear that my ship may go down and all that I know may go down with it. So that is why I am now sitting in my creaky little cabin writing this document.

And what will I do with it when I have finished it? I will do what others have done before me. I will place it in a well-sealed container and drop it into the waves. And with it will go my prayer that it may in time be picked up by human hands and read by human eyes.

Now why did Ibn Shaprut send my friend and me from Spain across to the other end of the European continent? I remember his words when he summoned us to the palace of his lord, the Sultan of Cordova. For Hasdai ibn Shaprut was the Sultan's chief minister and he received all his visitors in the royal palace.

"It is now certain," he told us, "that Khazaria is a Jewish kingdom. I have this assurance from the envoys of the monarchs of the East—of the Christian emperor who reigns in Constantinople and of the Sultan who reigns in Bagdad. Think of it, my friends! Today, nine hundred years after the Romans destroyed our Temple and scattered our people, there is a Jewish kingdom in the East, powerful enough to hold in check the heathen Russians on the north and the Christians and Moslems on the south. Is it possible for a Jewish heart not to be thrilled by this marvel?"

For a full minute Ibn Shaprut was silent. This great statesman, whose genius had lifted our people in Spain to honor and dignity, was too deeply moved to speak.

"But who are these Khazars?" he finally resumed. "Where do they hail from? Are they descended from our Lost Ten Tribes, or were they converted to our faith? If converted, when did it happen and how did it happen? To these questions, alas, I have no answers. They are like so many riddles that leave me no rest, and I am determined to solve them. I am especially anxious to know why, if they were able to choose, did they embrace our faith rather than the others? This, of course, is the most important question of all."

Ibn Shaprut beckoned us to come closer.

"Here is a letter," he went on, holding out a bound and sealed scroll. "I have written it in our holy tongue and it is addressed to King Joseph, who reigns over Khazaria. It contains all the questions I have just stated and others besides. To you, my friends, I entrust this letter, and I desire you to journey with it to Itil, the capital of the land of the Khazars. You will place it in the hands of the king and return to me with his reply."

So, with the blessings of our community, we left the stately city of Cordova, and began our long and rugged journey through the harsh lands of the north. We carried credentials from Ibn Shaprut in the name of our ruler. Without them, I am sure, we never would have reached our goal.

But I will not recount the details of our journey. Nor will I describe the rich land of the Khazars or the power and glory of the king who rules it from his palace in Itil. I will only say that the Khazars are brave warriors, but take no delight in battle and bloodshed. They prefer to cultivate their fields, tend their vineyards and raise cattle and horses.

Nor will I speak of the pomp and splendor with which

King Joseph received us or of his answers to the questions of Ibn Shaprut. I must, however, say something about his answer to the most important question of all.

The light which the king shed on the reasons why his people preferred the Jewish to the other faiths was hazy indeed. Their conversion, he stated, occurred in the reign of King Bulan, more than two hundred years ago. The king and his people still worshiped idols. King Bulan, who desired to adopt a higher faith, invited to his court learned Christians, Moslems and Jews who laid before him the merits of their respective beliefs. He then decided that the Jewish was the true faith and best suited for himself and his people. But on the reasons for his choice King Joseph shed no light at all.

As we stayed on in the capital of Khazaria my thirst for more knowledge of this encounter of the three religions grew and grew. My friend Isaac chose to stay within the precincts of the royal court, but I preferred to roam about in the broad city, to observe the people and the manner of their lives. And it happened that in one of these excursions I had the good fortune to come upon one who gave me the knowledge which I sought.

He was a man still in his prime, and when I first saw him he was leading a young lad by the hand, apparently his son. As I passed him I overheard him say something to the lad that startled me. The man spoke to his son in our holy tongue!

At once I drew near him and before long he became my fast friend. I had much to tell him about the lot of our people scattered in the lands around the Midland Sea, which he longed to hear.

My new friend, Uriah ben Shmuel, was a teacher of the laws and traditions of our faith. His father, his father's father, and all his ancestors as far back as he could trace them had also been teachers. His first ancestor in the land of the Khazars, whose name was Obadiah, had found refuge there from the persecutions of the Byzantine emperor, Leo III. And this Obadiah was the very man who, more than two hundred years ago, stood before King Bulan as the advocate and defender of the Jewish faith!

Since that distant day an exact knowledge of what happened during this encounter of the three creeds has been a kind of heirloom, going down from father to son in Uriah's family. I will now report in his own words what I heard from my friend in Itil.

The Christian emperor who ruled in Constantinople and the Moslem Sultan who ruled in Bagdad sent their best orators to Itil. The Jewish faith had no one at all to speak for it. It was, in fact, taken for granted that King Bulan would choose to become either a Christian or a Moslem. Besides, who was to send a Jewish advocate? There was no Jewish land or ruler to do it, and the Jewish communities of the East did not dare to do it. It would, they feared, bring fresh persecutions down upon them.

But the learned doctors from Constantinople and Bagdad did not come alone. Each of them was accompanied by a large contingent of followers who attended the debates, applauded their own champion and jeered at his opponent. It was not long before the debates became scenes of wrangling and disorder.

The opposing sides did not, however, stop there. They roamed the streets of Itil and when they met they clashed. Neither side, it seemed, had come unarmed, and on both sides there were wounded and slain.

King Bulan ordered a halt to the debate. He would not, he declared, permit it to resume until each side surrendered its weapons and pledged itself to keep the peace.

The weapons were surrendered, the pledges were given and the debate started afresh. But soon nough the wrangling and brawling also started afresh. Again there were clashes between the Christians and Moslems, and blood flowed in the streets and squares of the Khazar city.

The king was grieved and angry. He was also puzzled. Whence did these foreign guests of his obtain new weapons? he wondered. He called a meeting of his councillors and one of them, the oldest and wisest among them, spoke as follows:

"It is clear, Your Majesty, that our visitors have brought a larger supply of weapons than we thought, for none of your subjects would be so disloyal as to furnish them with weapons against your will. They have, of course, broken the pledge they gave us to surrender them. This breach of faith is contrary to the teachings of the religions which they urge us to embrace. But it seems to me, Your Majesty, that these men have come to us on a mission which is not religious at all."

The old councillor paused and waited for his lord to indicate that he might continue. King Bulan nodded.

"Let us never forget," the old councillor resumed, "that the Byzantine empire, whose rulers are Christians, and the countries lying east of it have rarely been at peace. They made war on each other when the countries to the east were ruled by the fire-worshipping Persians. They are making war on each other now when the rulers of those countries are Moslems. Both sides are looking for allies, and no other land attracts them so much as our own. If, therefore, we embrace the Christian faith, the Byzantine emperor is sure we will join him against the Moslems. If, on the other hand, we embrace the Moslem faith, the Sultan feels confident we will fight with him against the Christians.

"It is clear, therefore, that the mission of these guests of ours is not religious but political. They are using religion as a cloak to cover their real purpose. That is why they are so obstinate and bitter against each other. That is why they attack each other with deadly weapons in the streets of our peaceful city. I beg Your Majesty, therefore, to bid both return to their countries, and let us continue to worship our old gods."

King Bulan's expression grew more and more somber as the old councillor spoke.

"There is truth and wisdom in what you say," he declared. "But I am grieved that we must still cling to our ancient gods, for I am convinced they are false."

At this point the youngest of the councillors rose, and when he got leave to address the king he spoke as follows:

"I have listened to the champions of the two faiths who have come here to persuade us. They have said a great deal, but it seems to me they have left a great deal unsaid. Both of them have often referred to another and older faith, each of them claiming that his faith alone is its true heir and successor. But what this older faith is, they have not told us. They have left us with the notion that it is dead, since it now has an heir and successor. But, Your Majesty, I have learned that this older faith is not dead. It is, on the contrary, very much alive. It is the faith of the people, who, in ancient times, were called Hebrews, and who are today known as Jews.

"There are not many Jews dwelling in our land, Your Majesty, but I recently chanced to became acquainted with one of them. His name is Obadiah, which, in their ancient tongue means 'Servant of the Lord.' Obadiah fled to our land from Constantinople, where his people are being persecuted by the Byzantine ruler. His own land, he told me, was conquered by the Romans many centuries ago and his people are now scattered over the face of the earth. Their Gold, he told me, is the creator and ruler of heaven and earth and is worshiped with prayer and good deeds.

"I beg Your Majesty, therefore, to summon Obadiah to your court to explain the beliefs and practices of his faith. He will come with clean hands. He will come without a horde of armed followers. He will come without political designs. Perhaps we shall not have to worship pagan gods in whom we no longer believe."

It was in no happy frame that my ancestor, Obadiah, appeared before King Bulan and his councillors. He was a God-fearing man and mindful of the warning of our sages not to hobnob with the ruling powers. But he was not a faintheart, and when he stood before them he spoke clearly and boldly. He began by explaining that the Jewish faith was not eager to make converts. On the other hand, it welcomed those who accepted its commands and obligations. They plied him with questions, which he answered without trying to please them or lure them into his creed.

He told them of our people's great past, of the Patriarchs, of Moses and Joshua, of David and Solomon, of our prophets and sages. He appeared before them again and again.

"Obadiah," the king said finally, "your words have touched my heart. They are simple and noble. So, indeed, is the creed for which you speak. I desire therefore that you appear before the spokesmen of the other faiths and defend yours against them. Have no fear of them or their followers. I will assign a sufficient guard to protect you and you will not be harmed. Be strong and of good courage. Aren't those the words which Moses spoke to Joshua?"

There is little more that needs to be told. When the other two saw that the new contender was gaining the upper hand, they united against him. They even made a desperate attempt to put him out of the way. In the principal square of Itil, there took place what might be called a pitched battle. But their ruffians were no match for the king's guard.

The following day the Christian and Moslem champions, together with their followers, began their journey back, each to his own country. And King Bulan and his councillors, as well as the leading men of Khazaria and large numbers of the common people, became converts to the Jewish faith.

I, Nathan ben Ezra, attest that the above is a true report

When he stood before them he spoke clearly and boldly

of what my friend, Uriah ben Shmuel, a descendant of
Obadiah, told me. I will now seal what I have written in
the silver tube which I have ready, and drop it into the
sea. If God grants me to reach Cordova safely, I will report
these matters to Ibn Shaprut. If not, this tube will perhaps

be plucked from the waves and the truth will be known.

One thing more I have just remembered. Many years after King Bulan a Khazar king whose devotion to the Jewish faith was strong and deep, sought a name for himself that would express his zeal. The name he chose was Obadiah.

THE GREAT HEALER

Joseph ben Nathan came from London, England. Samuel ibn Gad came from Cairo, Egypt. Would anyone have guessed that the two would ever meet? And where, of all places, did they meet? In Palestine, the land where the remote ancestors of both had lived many centuries before. To be more exact, they met a little more than eleven centuries after those ancestors had been driven from the land by the conquering Romans.

All that is strange enough. But the way they met is even stranger. They did not meet as friends but as foes! Joseph of London was in the service of Richard Lionheart, the English king who had come to Palestine on a Crusade. His aim was to wrest the Holy Land from the Moslems, the "unbelievers," as the Christians called them. Samuel of Cairo was in the service of Saladin, the Sultan of Egypt, Palestine and neighboring lands, whom Richard was fighting.

Richard had gone off on this Crusade with Philip Augustus, the king of France and Frederick Redbeard, the German king, pious Christians all three of them. But the three had no love for one another.

Poor Redboard dropped out of the partnership rather early: he was drowned before he got to Palestine. Over in Germany people wouldn't believe that he was dead. He was fast asleep, they said, in a cave up on a mountain. His fiery beard, they said, kept on growing and it grew right through a stone slab near which he was sitting. At the right moment he would wake up and make Germany great and powerful. How he was going to pull his beard out of the slab they didn't say.

The remaining partners, Richard and Philip, kept it up for a time. But they were always quarreling. Finally Philip got tired of it all and went back to France. There he plotted against his former ally with John, Richard's own brother.

So there was Richard left alone to carry on the Crusade against Saladin. But now came the queerest thing of all. Richard and Saladin fought each other, but at the same time they respected and admired each other. They were both brave and gallant men. Richard esteemed the "unbeliever" more than he did his Christian partners.

But how did it happen that Joseph of London, who was also an "unbeliever," though not a Moslem but a Jew, was in the service of a crusading monarch? This was strange indeed because the Jews of England were being cruelly persecuted at the time. The answer is that Joseph, who was a merchant and had visited many countries and knew many languages, including Arabic, was drafted into the Crusade to serve as Richard's interpreter and scribe. Could Joseph have refused the "honor" of being a "crusader"? Not if he valued his life. But Richard did excuse him from wearing the cross on his outer garment, which every crusader wore. In fact, Richard himself was not a persecutor. In England, as in other lands, it was the clergy who fanned the flames of persecution against the Jews.

As for Samuel of Cairo, he didn't have to be drafted. He, like all his people, believed that in time Palestine would be restored to the Jews. But if, in the meantime, the country had to be ruled by others, they preferred the rulers to be Moslems rather than Christians. In the main, the Moslems were not such pitiless persecutors. So Joseph, like other young men of his faith who lived in Egypt, became soldiers of the Sultan Saladin.

Richard Lionheart established his headquarters in Jaffa on the coast of Palestine. North, east and south of the city, he built strong redoubts to prevent the Moslems from storming it. But to all intents and purposes he himself was cooped up in it. Occasionally a unit of his men sallied out and, after skirmishing with the enemy, retired behind their fortifications. Those were probing actions, aimed to discover weak spots in the enemy's deployment. Another aim was to bring back prisoners, and the duty of questioning them fell upon Joseph of London.

It happened one day that Joseph questioned a prisoner who gave his name as Samuel and the place of his birth as Cairo. The conversation, of course, was in Arabic.

"I shall ask you a few more questions," said Joseph sternly, "and I advise you to answer truthfully. If you don't, we have ways of extracting the truth, which you will not find pleasant. Why do you stare at me like that?"

"Forgive me," Samuel apologized. "But—" he stopped and stared again. Was it possible? he asked himself.

"Speak!" Joseph ordered.

"There is something—something about the way you speak Arabic," Samuel tried to explain, "that tells me—." Again he hesitated.

"Tells you what?" Joseph demanded.

"That it's more natural for you to speak Hebrew."

When the two men recovered from their surprise, they resumed their conversation, but not in Arabic. It lasted a long time. There was so much each of them wanted to know—not, however, about military matters.

"How do our people fare in your country?" Samuel asked.

"Until two years ago things were not too bad for us," Joseph replied. "We were the wards of the king and he protected us against the rabble. But when Richard was crowned there were bloody outbreaks against us. And all because a group of our leading men came to the coronation with gifts for the king. But it was not Richard's fault," he hastened to add. "It was the fault of the churchmen. They incited the populace against us. I left shortly afterwards with the king's forces. I had no choice. But I have since learned of the bloody events that took place in London, in York and other towns."

"And how have you fared in the service of the king—a Jew among a host of crusaders?"

"It may surprise you, but I have been treated well. The king himself saw to that."

"You are fond of King Richard, aren't you?"

"I confess I am. But the poor king has been ill now for some time. He has a burning fever and his doctors are unable to help him."

Samuel was silent awhile.

"Moses ben Maimon could help him," he finally declared. "We, his own people, know that Moses is the greatest teacher and philosopher of our time, but all men say he is the king of physicians."

Joseph's face lighted up.

"Perhaps he will come here," he spoke eagerly. "How can he be persuaded, Samuel? His reward would be great. Of that I can assure you."

"Moses ben Maimon," said Samuel, "would not be lured by the kind of reward you have in mind. But there is a serious difficulty. He is the official physician of our Sultan Saladin and his court in Cairo. He would not feel free to come here unless he had the Sultan's permission."

Both men sat silent and thoughtful.

"It may be possible," said Joseph at last, "to overcome the difficulty. Richard and Saladin are not ordinary enemies. They are both generous and noble men and they respect each other. I will go to my king and ask him to release you with a message to Saladin, which I will write myself. You will deliver it to the Sultan and I believe he will grant the permission we seek."

This is the reply from Saladin which Samuel brought back for Richard.

"My dear enemy: The news of your illness has made me sad. Do you not agree with me that you should never have come to this country? The fogs and damps of London were kinder to you than the bright sunlight of Palestine. When all is said and done, a man's native country is best suited for him. This truth should persuade you to set sail for England without delay. You know I think highly of you, but I will not be sorry to see you go.

"But no more jesting. I do hope that this physician, Moses ben Maimon, would come and heal you. He is of the stock of Abraham and the prophets, whom you and I also hold in reverence. This reminds me that your faith and mine have been called daughters of Judaism. I don't think the daughters can take pride in the way they have treated their mother, do you?

"Moses ben Maimon, as you know from your prisoner, is held in the highest esteem, not only as a healer, but as a man of vast learning and wisdom. Some call him Maimonides, as a mark of honor. Our own sages and philosophers look up to him as their master. My Jewish subjects regard him as second only to Moses the lawgiver. I cannot dispose of him as I would of an ordinary man. Not even I, his sovereign, can order him to go here or there.

"My advice, therefore, is that you dispatch two trusted messengers to Cairo to carry your invitation to him. I send you, along with this letter, two safe-conducts for them. Moses ben Maimon will then feel free to go or not to go. And my safe-conducts will make it clear to him that I, for my part, will not object if he accepts your invitation.

"May your health be speedily restored and may the day come soon when we can meet as friends, not as foes."

The next day Joseph and Samuel boarded a small sloop for Egypt, King Richard having consented that the two should be his messengers to Maimonides. Two days later they reached Damietta, the nearest Egyptian port on the Mediterranean. The following day they arrived in Cairo and were received by Moses ben Maimon.

They had to wait several hours before the great healer and sage could receive them. They were amazed to see the throngs that waited in his anteroom. Nor did all of them come to be cured of their ills. Some came to consult him on the affairs of the Jewish community in Egypt of which he was the head. Others were there as emissaries from Jewish communities in other lands with questions on Talmudic law, which they felt only he could answer. Still others, among them learned Moslems and Christians who had read and studied his works, came for the privilege of meeting their master face to face. But he gave most of his time to those who came to be relieved of their sufferings.

Moses ben Maimon glanced at the safe-conducts of his sovereign and read the letter from the King of England. The letter was more than a call to visit a patient. It hinted that Richard was prepared to appoint him his personal physician. On this matter Moses made up his mind promptly. He would pay no attention to the hint.

"The king's letter will require much thought," he said to the two messengers. "Come again tomorrow and I will give you my reply."

Before dismissing them, however, he questioned Joseph at length about the king's illness. But he spent even more time informing himself on the lot of his people in the domains of King Richard. To Samuel he said: "God bless you and keep you, my son, and may this war come to a speedy end."

This is the reply which Maimonides handed Joseph on the morrow and which, some days later, Joseph read to his king:

"To His Majesty, Richard Plantagent, King of England, Duke of Aquitania and Normandy, etc.:

"Sire: I am mindful of the honor which your invitation has conferred upon me, and I have spent anxious hours pondering the proper course for me to follow. The wishes

Moses ben Maimon read the letter from the King of England

of a monarch, even of one who does not command one's allegiance, are not to be treated lightly.

"After praying that Heaven direct my heart to the right choice, it became clear to me that my duty to the royal court and to the many patients who look to me for help, forbids me to leave this city. Fortunately, the choice became less difficult after I questioned your faithful servant, Joseph, who informed me of your condition and symptoms. I am fully satisfied as to the cause and nature of your ailment. I have provided him with the necessary medication, and have given him clear instructions. He can be trusted to follow them, and I am confident that your health will soon be restored.

"Perhaps it has not escaped the attention of Your Majesty that both your messengers belong to the faith from which your own is sprung. The land where you are at this moment once belonged to the children of this faith, and with God's favor it will again belong to them. This our prophets have foretold. This you may read in the Holy Scriptures, which are holy to you also. All the victories which you may win will not avail against God's purpose.

"I beg Your Majesty to consider, therefore, if the wars which Christians are still waging for the recovery of this land should not be brought to an end. These wars have brought untold misery upon the Christians themselves. They have also brought suffering to the people of other faiths. Thousands of my own faith were cruelly slain in Europe during the First Crusade a hundred years ago. In your own country many of them fell victims to the insane fury of mobs after you sailed away on the present Crusade. You and my sovereign should have no difficulty reaching an honorable agreement. I know he is well disposed towards you and you towards him.

"You will then be able to return to your own country and devote yourself to the welfare of your people. Let there be no more crusades against other people. I implore you to launch, instead, a crusade against hate and misery. Such a crusade will be more pleasing to God, the father of us all, than the crusades that have drenched the Holy Land, and other lands also, with the blood of His children."

"Joseph," said Samuel to his friend some time later,

"how is the king? Are the remedies helping him?"

"Indeed they are," Joseph replied. "It will not be long, I am sure, before his health is restored."

"And what of the letter, Joseph? Has the king taken it to heart? Will he now cease from war and bloodshed?"

Joseph looked long at his friend and smiled sadly.

"Samuel," he finally said, "I know that Richard and Saladin will soon patch up a peace. But this disease of war and bloodshed, from which my king and other kings suffer, will take much longer to cure. Some day, we must hope, the cure will come. Didn't the prophet Isaiah, declare it? Didn't he say: 'They shall beat their swords into ploughshares, and their spears into pruning-hooks?'"

HAMAN AT THE FEAST

hy isn't he at his post, Our Haman?" Hershel the *shammes* wondered as he drove through the gate of the Romburg ghetto.

It was early morning of the day before Purim, and Hershel, with horse and cart, was on his way to the town beyond the gate. It was high time for him to put in supplies for the beggars' feast which he provided every Purim night.

Hershel reined in his nag and peered through the tiny window of the hut near the gate. He was a little man, with a broad black beard and lively eyes. His long glossy coat came down to his ankles and flapped about him as he walked.

"He is not in the gatehouse, either," the *shammes* continued to wonder. "Where can he be, Our Haman? In the tavern so early in the morning?"

"Our Haman" was one of two nicknames which the people of the ghetto of Romburg conferred on the keeper of the gate. His real name was Schickel and his other nickname was Shikker. The change was slight, but it meant a great deal, *Shikker* being the Hebrew word for drunkard. Both nicknames suited the gatekeeper remarkably well. Schickel was a big hulk of a man, with a flat blotchy face, broad stooping shoulders and arms that came down to his knees. He walked like a gorilla and growled like one, his growls being directed at the people of the ghetto. All of them, he felt, were his personal enemies, so he made no secret of the fact that he was their sworn foe. They soon discovered there was only one means to take the edge off the malice of Our Haman: to ply him with strong drink till he sank into a dead stupor. It was a costly means, for Shikker needed much more liquor than the ordinary tippler to arrive at that blissful state.

Schikel's principal duty was to lock the heavy gate of the ghetto at sundown and open it at sunrise. For the ghetto of Romburg was like the many other ghettos of Europe in those centuries, the centuries known as the Middle Ages. The people who were forced to live in them had to be back in their homes before dark and were not allowed to leave the ghetto before sunrise.

Like the others, also, the Romburg ghetto consisted of a walled street, at one end of which lay the burial ground and at the other stood the grim iron-studded gate. The largest building among the gabled houses that rose on each side of the narrow street was, of course, the synagogue.

Hershel put the gatekeeper out of his mind and drove on. The *shammes* had other things to think about, all of them having to do with the jolly festival which would begin that night. He checked them off in his mind as his cart clattered along on the cobblestones of the town's principal street.

Hershel felt satisfied. Every Purim player knew his lines and had his costume patched up and ready. There were plenty of rattles and other noise-makers for the boys to "welcome" Haman properly when his name is heard during the reading of the Megillah in the synagogue. And every messenger who carried the Purim gifts from neighbor to neighbor knew which families "belonged" to him. And now he was off to buy and bring home whatever he still lacked for the beggars' Purim feast.

The ghetto of Romburg agreed that the merit and glory of this event belonged to Hershel alone. The ghetto, of course, had its own share of beggars, but the fame of this feast had spread far and wide. Many beggars from other ghettos filtered in, and became uninvited but welcome guests at Hershel's Purim board.

They were a queer but wonderful lot, with beggars of every size, shape and attire. As they ate and drank their spirits rose and overflowed. Under Hershel's direction they sang songs in praise of Mordecai and in scorn of Haman. They clapped hands and danced around the table. Some did solo parts, imitating wheezy old cantors and stuttering preachers. Others showed their skill at imitating the barnyard birds and beasts, clucking and crowing, barking and meowing, mooing and neighing. The beggars hugged each other, shaking and roaring with laughter. At Hershel's Purim feast nothing was barred that would heighten the joy of his guests.

"They deserve it, poor folk," Hershel mused as he jolted over the cobblestones. "Don't they also belong to God's chosen people? Our lot in this long and bitter exile is hard enough, but theirs is especially hard."

Hershel looked ahead and saw something that made him pull at the reins and slow down his horse's pace. He was approaching the tavern, and at its door stood a large group of men with the huge bulk of the gatekeeper in the center. Two or three of them were talking earnestly to Schickel who stood silent, lolling and nodding his head.

"That's quite a gathering," Hershel decided, "and I don't like their looks. And what is Our Haman doing among them?"

A marked change came over the group as Hershel came closer. The men fell silent and glowered at him as he passed. Hershel felt a sudden sinking of the heart. He and, indeed, all his people, had learned to read the signs that spelled danger.

The people who lived inside the ghettos had few friends among the outsiders. Most of them, and especially the rabble in the towns, eyed them with envy and malice. Wild stories were afloat, which the rabble believed, that every dweller in the ghetto was rich, with hidden treasures stored away in secret places. The ghetto owed its safety principally to the ruler of the city, whether prince, baron or bishop. He regarded the Jews as his "personal property," for they paid him well for the right to live in his realm. As a rule, therefore, he protected them against the malice of the mob.

"Shall I go to the prince's palace and tell the captain of the guard what I have seen?" Hershel asked himself. "But what will I tell him? That some men near the tavern looked at me as if they didn't like me? The captain will only laugh at me."

The *shammes* drove on and piled up on his cart the things he came for. He bought two stout sacks of potatoes, two more of white flour, a good supply of poppy seeds, prunes, sugar and onions, as well as cinnamon, pepper and other spices. Meat and wine he had already bought in the ghetto; they, of course, had to be kosher.

He was about to turn and drive back when an idea crossed his mind. He stopped and put in a big supply of strong drink. "I don't know just how," said he to himself, "but these bottles may prove useful." He was obeying what is sometimes called a "hunch".

As he passed through the gate into the ghetto he obeyed still another impulse. He stepped into the gatehouse and found Schickel at his midday meal.

"Schickel," said the *shammes,* producing a bottle from the pocket of his long, flapping coat, "take a little swig and tell me how you like it."

Schickel did not wait to be urged. He took a long pull, then a few more until the bottle was nearly empty. His face turned red and he grunted with satisfaction.

"Good!" he declared.

"It's for my Purim feast tomorrow night," Hershel explained. "Whoever comes will have as much as he can drink."

"Tomorrow night? Tomorrow night?" the gatekeeper mumbled.

"Yes, tomorrow night," Hershel assured him.

Something resembling a smile appeared on Schickel's flat face. He leaned back and a strange gleam shone in his little eyes.

"A feast for you tomorrow night. Yes, yes," he grunted. "A feast!" Then he spluttered out something that could have been taken for a laugh.

Hershel, who knew Our Haman well, had never seen him so jovial.

"Keep the bottle," he told the gateman as he stepped out.

He was now sure that a grave danger hung over the ghetto, and that it was set to strike on Purim night.

The following night Hershel's attic, where the beggars' feast took place, was more crowded and noisy than ever. The guests had everything to make them happy. They ate as if they had been fasting for weeks, and drowned their cares in the spiced meed which Hershel's wife had brewed for them. They began to clamor for the stunts that always followed the meal, when Hershel stood up and silenced them.

"Good friends," he said. "Tonight we rejoice at the downfall of the Persian Haman, who plotted to destroy us. So may all other Hamans be brought down and their plans come to nought. I leave you now for a little while, and when I return our feast will be merrier than ever."

The beggars were puzzled. Why the sudden departure of their host? Whatever the reason, it must be important. Some of them began to feel uneasy.

In less than a minute Hershel covered the short distance to the gatehouse, and entered boldly without knocking. Schickel was sitting on his cot, more sulky than usual.

"Schickel," the beadle called out cheerily, holding out a large amber-colored bottle, "I've brought you something from my Purim feast."

The gatekeeper eyed the bottle gloomily.

"I can't, not tonight!" he blurted out.

"Behold! Haman himself has come to our Purim feast!"

"You promised not to?" said Hershel casually.

"They made me promise," Schickel snarled, his face red with sudden rage.

Hershel uncorked the bottle.

"They didn't say you mustn't smell it, did they?" he

laughed, bringing the bottle to Schickel's nose.

The gatekeeper's huge frame trembled. He snatched the bottle and emptied it in a single gulp.

"More!" he demanded.

The beadle produced another bottle and its contents followed the same road.

"More! More!" Schickel rasped.

"No more. I've brought no more," the beadle replied.

"You—you—" the huge man growled, half rising from the cot. But the next moment he plumped down again and a flood of tears came rolling down from his little red eyes.

"One more," he slobbered. "One little bottle more. I— I—"

"Then come with me," said Hershel. "Come and I'll give you more and more and more."

Schickel lumbered along after the *shammes,* and when the two appeared in the attic, the beggars stared with bulging eyes and open mouths. Hershel led his new guest to a place of honor, stood up on a chair and shouted:

"Behold! Haman himself has come to our Purim feast!"

The words were like a signal which all the beggars understood. They welcomed Our Haman with the strangest broadside that was ever heard. Shrieks and whistles mingled with the yelping of dogs, the crowing of roosters and the neighing of horses.

But the guest of honor himself seemed either unaware of the enthusiasm he aroused or indifferent to it. He sat down and emptied one beaker after another which the beadle kept filling for him. At last the uproar began to wane and at the same time the gatekeeper was seen to slump down lower and lower. At last he disappeared from the chair and a loud thud was heard under the table. The event was greeted by a whoop of delight.

But in the silence that followed new and wholly different sounds made themselves heard. The gate of the ghetto was being heavily pounded. The blows grew louder and more frequent. At the same time hoarse shouts reached the ears of Hershel's guests. They stood up looking mutely at each other, and faces that were flushed with good cheer turned suddenly white.

Hershel stood up on his chair, holding high over his head an iron ring from which hung a number of large keys.

"Have no fear!" he cried. "The gate is securely locked. We have the keys and we have the keyman." He was about to tell them more when the pounding came to a sudden stop. In its place there was a rapid stamping as of many feet in flight, followed by the drumming of galloping hoofs.

"The prince's horsemen!" Hershel cried. "How lucky we are to have a Haman who loves the bottle!"

The following day the joker of the ghetto, the *letz,* as they called him, came up with a new riddle.

"What is the difference," he asked the people, "between the Haman of the Megillah and Our Haman?"

"You tell us!" they all cried.

"It's simple," he assured them. "The Haman of the Megillah was hanged. Our Haman was drowned."

OUT OF THE DEPTHS

The exiles clung to each other, huddled together in the hold of the vessel like sheep in a storm. But one of them, the youthful Judah Medigo, held aloof from the rest. He sat peering at the gaunt faces of the bearded men, at the pale-faced women and the frightened children they clasped in their arms.

He listened at the same time to a white-bearded man of noble aspect who was speaking to them.

"Remember what we said to each other when they drove us into exile," the old patriarch was telling them. "Let us go forth, we said, in the name of the Lord. The Lord, my children, is still with us. In His hands—"

But it was not easy to hear everything he said. For every now and then a wilder blast of the storm that raged outside sent a shudder through the little ship, and his words were lost. His aim, however, was plain enough. It was to strengthen the hearts of these wanderers in the dire peril they were facing.

They were a group of refugees fleeing from Spain, the land which they and all their people had been ordered to leave. Several days earlier they had boarded the small craft in the harbor of Barcelona and set sail for Salonika. The Turkish Sultan was welcoming the fugitives from Spain, and Salonika lay within his empire.

On the fourth day they rounded Cape Malea at the tip of one of the legs that Greece stretches out into the Mediterranean. They turned north into the Aegean Sea, picking their way through the cluster of islands called the Cyclades. Another day or two and the vessel would be safe in the harbor of Salonika.

Then the storm came down like a rabid monster. The giant waves tossed the vessel about like a piece of drift-wood. Her sails had all been furled, her mast cut down, and her rudder was useless. At any moment the ship might crash on one of the rocks or islands and break into splinters.

They were a brave and proud people, these exiles. There were men among them who had stood high in wealth and power. Judah Medigo knew it was not their habit to stand idle in the face of danger. But this time they were helpless and they knew it.

Strange memories spring up in grim moments like these. The sun-bathed city of Gerona where he was born rose suddenly before Judah Medigo. His father had been the leading physician of the city, and Judah was preparing for the same calling. How bright and full of promise his life lay before him!

The next moment he recalled the herald of King Ferdinand and Queen Isabella who read the order of expulsion in the large square of the city. All Jews found on Spanish soil after a stated day would, unless they gave up their faith, suffer death.

There was no panic. His people were too proud to give way to despair. They prepared for exile and tried to sell their possessions. They had to barter a house for a cart, a vineyard for a donkey. Only at the cemetery, where they came to take leave of their precious dead, did they give vent to their grief. Then they boarded the overcrowded ships that took them away from the land they loved, the land where their people had lived for a thousand years.

Again Judah Medigo heard the voice of the old man.

"Whatever befalls us, let us remember, my children, to bless the Lord and sanctify His Name. For he chose us among all the nations—"

The voice halted, and this time it was not the storm that silenced it. Another voice broke from the huddled group, a harsh and shrill voice that rose above the bellow of the gale and the creaking of the hold.

"He chose us, did you say?" the voice rasped. "Yes, He chose us for sorrow and suffering! He chose us to receive evil for good. How we labored for the glory and greatness of Spain! We brought her wealth and honor, we fought for her, we died for her. Do you know it was we who enabled this Italian navigator they call Columbus to set out on his voyage? His proud ships sailed off the very day we boarded this rickety boat to go into exile. More glory and power for Spain! And for us? Listen to the storm! This boat is breaking up! We are doomed, we are—"

Angry voices rose up from the group, shouting the speaker down. But the man's bitter words could not be erased. The lofty and pious mood of the exiles was spoiled. In his own heart Judah heard a little voice that whispered "He is right! The man is right!" Some of the women broke into weeping and the children in their arms whimpered and wailed.

Judah Medigo found it too painful to stay in the hold. He crawled to the hatch and toiled up the companionway to the deck. The sailors were huddled together in the forecastle, straining their eyes into the distance.

Clinging to every possible support, Judah managed to join the group, but tried in vain to make out what lay ahead. Before him was nothing but a chaos of driving clouds and waves.

But a new sound reached his ears and it grew louder and louder. It was a hoarse and sullen roar as of a pack of hungry wolves. Then something appeared to the sight, a white line on the horizon that grew rapidly longer as the ship drove towards it. Soon the roar of breakers almost silenced the shrieking of the gale.

Cries rose up from the sailors.

"It's the coast of Andros!"

"With Tenos to starboard!"

"And the narrow channel between them!"

They raised their arms and shouted in a frenzy of joy

"We're being driven on Andros!'
"No, on Tenos!"
"Heaven have mercy! We are lost!"
The vessel continued driving swiftly towards Andros.
But suddenly the coastline seemed to veer away to port and

the bow pointed to open water. The ship was rushing clear through the narrow channel between the two islands! It raced swiftly between the churning breakers on either side and lunged into the broad sea beyond.

For a moment the sailors were mute with awe. Then they flung themselves on their knees, raised their arms and shouted in a frenzy of joy.

Judah made his way back to the hold where the exiles, who heard the roar of the breakers, were silently praying.

"The ship is safe!' he cried. "It drove through the channel between the two islands.!"

In the night the storm abated. The sailors repaired the rudder and set up the mast. After two more days the vessel, under full sail, reached the port of Salonika.

On the landing Judah Medigo stood near the old man. He was about to speak to him, when one of the exiles came near.

"Master," he said, "forgive me. I am the man who scorned your words. I spoke in anger and despair."

"Go in peace, my son," the old man replied.

In the trials of the voyage Judah had lost the reckoning of the days.

"Master, what day have we today?" he asked the patriarch.

"Friday," the man informed him.

"Friday," Judah repeated. "We sailed on the Ninth of Ab. So tomorrow is the Sabbath of Consolation."

"Yes," came the answer. "Tomorrow we read in Isaiah, 'Comfort ye, comfort ye, my people.' "

EACH TO HIS OWN

zra Mendes pounded on the gate of the Wall that stood between New Amsterdam and its enemies. "Open up!" he cried. "It's me, Ezra Mendes, and I have a prisoner!"

"A prisoner?" shouted Willem Hooten, the captain of the guard. "Don't you know we don't take prisoners? Shoot him before we open the gate!"

"I can't, Captain," Ezra pleaded. 'Let me through and do it yourself, if you must!"

Ezra Mendes came through the gate with his "prisoner" hanging limp over his shoulder.

"Who is this?" the captain growled. "Where did you find him? Is he alive or dead?"

Ezra laid his burden down carefully on the ground.

"He's still alive, Captain," he said. "I found him in the brush, about half a mile north. He has a bad wound in his leg and has lost a lot of blood."

The captain peered closely at the figure on the ground.

"A mere stripling," he snarled "and already a scalping savage. Mohican, of course. Why did you have to bring him in?" he turned on Ezra. "Shoot him, or else I will!"

"Captain," Ezra pleaded, "I beg you— I beg you—"

The captain raised his blunderbuss to his shoulder, but before he could fire, a hand reached out from behind him and jerked up the barrel skyward. The captain turned about, trembling with rage.

"Ah!" he cried, "it's you, Asser Levy!"

"And not a second too soon," the man replied, his voice calm and ironic.

"How dare you!" the captain thundered. "Your insol-

ence grows from day to day! I warned the governor not
to admit you into the guard. Now more of your tribe have
come in, this—this young idiot for example! But I'll show
you who is in command here!"

The Dutchman moved a few steps away and made ready
to aim his firearm again.

"Don't, Captain!" Asser Levy called out sharply.
"There'll be many of your own tribe who will not approve!"

Slowly the captain lowered the stock of his blunderbuss
to the the ground.

"Young or old, you are a hard lot to take," he jeered.
"What do you plan to do with this savage? He'll be dead
before the morning, in any case."

"Give him to me!" cried Ezra lifting the Indian boy to
his shoulder. "Asser Levy, run to David Coronel and tell
him to come to my home at once! Pull him out of bed if
he's asleep!"

The physician, David Coronel, found the Indian's thigh-
bone broken just above the knee.

"I can set the bone easily enough" he said, "but it will
take a long time and a lot of nursing to restore his strength."

"We will do our best," said Ezra's mother.

When Miriam Mendes first saw the wan face of the
Indian youth her heart was wrung with pity. At the same
time a strange thought flashed through her mind.

"He is so handsome, this youth. We will make him
strong and, perhaps—who knows?—he will be a brother
to Ezra."

Ezra, who was his mother's only child, was nimble
cub of nine when he arrived in New Amsterdam in 1654
with the first group of Jewish settlers, and in the ten years
that followed he had picked up a good deal of the Mohican
language. But for weeks all his efforts to make his "prisoner" talk were wasted. Only his eyes spoke, and what they
first expressed was fear and distrust. Later, when he became stronger, they glittered with anger and challenge

whenever Ezra or the doctor came near him. He was like a creature of the woods, at once shrinking and defiant.

"Mother," Ezra once remarked. "Have you noticed how he glares at me? But when you appear his eyes soften. Yet he must know that I saved his life."

"Patience," his mother replied.

Several weeks passed and the lad was able to sit up. And early one morning when Ezra entered his room, he found him lying near the door, helpless and panting. He raised him up in his arms and laid him down on the bed.

"So you were going to run away," he said.

Nearly six weeks later the great change took place. It was kindness that subdued him finally; it succeeded in doing what no enemy could have done. His face lighted up whenever Ezra's mother came near him, and in the end his trust in her reached out to her son.

His name, he told them, was Red Beaver and he was the son of a brother of Soaring Eagle, the chief of the Mohican tribe that had its council fire on the island of Shodac near Fort Orange. The braves with whom he paddled down the river towards New Amsterdam were not a scalping party. The Mohicans had not been attacking the white settlers for many years. The party had come down with a cargo of pelts in the hope of exchanging them for firearms against a more dangerous enemy: the Mohawks and their allies. At one place where they halted, Red Beaver had strayed too far from the bank. He heard the blast of a blunderbuss and fell to the ground, unable to move.

"Now," he said to Ezra in conclusion, "I must return to my people. Will you help me?"

"Stay with us and be my brother," said Ezra.

"I must return to my people," the Indian repeated calmly.

Red Beavers' decision was a hard blow to Miriam Mendes. She consulted with Asser Levy.

"Of course you must let him go!" Asser Levy boomed.

"Do you think you can raise a fawn of the woods in your parlor? But I dont' know how you will get him over to his tribe, Ezra. There are rumors in the settlement that the Mohawks have driven the Mohicans from their hunting grounds. Most of them, it seems, have fled to Westenhuck in Massachusetts, where kinsmen of theirs have their council fire."

The rumors, alas, proved to be true. How, now, was Red Beaver to rejoin his tribe in its new home? Ezra went for advice to every trapper in the settlement. They agreed that a journey by canoe would be least dangerous, and in a few days Ezra completed his preparations.

They set out on a morning of mid-July from a point south of the Wall where the East River mingles with the Upper Bay. They paddled up the River, skirting close· to the Manhattan shore, for on Long Island the British had outposts, and they were not friendly to the Dutch settlers. They swung into Long Island Sound and camped for the night on its northern shore near the mouth of the Housatonic River. The following morning they glided up the sparkling stream and before nightfall reached the encampment at Westenhuck.

The return of the chief's nephew brought the braves to the council fire for a joyous celebration, which lasted more than a week. Ezra had to extend his stay with the tribe; to leave too soon would have been a discourtesy. Finally, after nearly two weeks, he was called to stand before Soaring Eagle and a group of his seasoned warriors.

"My son," said the chief, "hear what we have decided. Our hearts overflow with gratitude for your brave deeds. We will therefore adopt you, and you will become one of our nation."

It took Ezra a full minute before he was able to speak.

"Noble father of a noble nation," he said, "could I do a thing that Red Beaver was unable to do? I pray you to let him explain."

Ezra was called to stand before Soaring Eagle

Red Beaver's explanation was followed by a long silence. Then the chief and his retinue whispered together. Finally Soaring Eagle laid his hand on Ezra's shoulder.

"It grieves me to part with you," he said. "But they tell me you already belong to an ancient and noble people. Go back to them with our greetings of peace."

An escort of three long canoes filled with Mohican braves accompanied Ezra to the mouth of the Housatonic. On a morning in early August he pulled his canoe up on the shore of Manhattan. The same day some of the leading men of the Jewish community in New Amsterdam came to welcome him home.

He had hardly begun to speak of his journey when Asser Levy burst into the room.

"News! News!" he shouted. "Three English warships have cast anchor in the harbor! They demand the surrender of the settlement. Poor Peter Peg-leg! He'll have to yield. What else can he do?"

It took a little while before the excitement was over and Ezra could tell his story.

"In time, Ezra, you could have become a big Indian chief," said the physician David Coronel.

When the laughter was over Asser Levy's voice boomed out again.

"In this New World," he declared, "there will be many peoples and many faiths. No man will have to forsake and deny his own, as many of our people are forced to do in the Old World. Here they will learn to respect one another and live in peace."

"Well spoken! Bravo, Asser Levy!" the others cried.

THE RIDE OF THE TENTH

here are times, of course, when it's hard to bring together ten worshipers to make up a *minyan,* and without this quorum of ten, as everybody knows, we cannot pray together as a group. In the course of my long life I have often been drafted to be the tenth man, but the story I want to tell you is about a *minyan* to which I rushed of my own accord, nearly losing my life before I got to it.

I must begin with my father, peace to his soul. My father was a man of action. At a time when others talked and dreamed, he acted. He was, for example, the first in his little town in Russia to pack up and migrate to America. That was in the early eighties of the last century when the Jews in Russia were the victims of savage pogroms and other persecutions. In those years and in the years that followed hundreds of thousands of them flocked to America and found refuge there.

In America, thank God, there were no pogroms and no police raids. In America all men were equal before the law, no matter how they worshiped God. But did that mean that, for those early newcomers, America was a land of milk and honey? Alas, no. Most of them toiled long and weary hours in dismal shops to earn the barest living for themselves and their children. Sweatshops, they called them. And they lived in dark and crowded tenements which the sun, it seemed, forgot to visit.

I remember the day when my father came home happy and excited, and spoke just three words: "I did it!"

We—my mother, my two brothers, my sister Ruth and I —knew what he meant. We had been talking about it for months, perhaps for years. We knew he had bought a farm! We also knew that practically all our precious savings had gone into the down payment.

Our neighbors also talked and dreamed about being farmers. They talked about the ancient days when their ancestors tilled the soil and tended their flocks in their own sunny land, the Land of Israel. "What have we here?" they used to sigh. "Walls and back yards and stone pavements. No grass, no trees, no sunlight." They even sang songs about plowing and planting and reaping. I remember one in particular that began with the lines:

> *To plow the soil—*
> *What blessed toil!*

In a matter of five or six weeks we, at least, had turned our backs on the lower East Side of New York—the "Ghetto," as it was called. We were living on a farm in New Jersey, "under God's glowing sky," as my father was fond of saying. It took much longer, of course, before we could call our venture a success. Fortunately, my father was still in his prime, and my brothers and I were brawny lads, eager to work and quick to learn.

My mother and sister, I must say, found the new life at first rather hard and lonely. In those days the automobile was barely known. There were no movies, no radio, no television. The telephone was a luxury which only the rich could afford. In the end, however, my father's energy and enthusiasm conquered them also. The first blossoms on our apple trees or the birth of a new calf became wonderful events for Ruth and my mother also.

There was one thing, however, which my father sorely missed. It was impossible to assemble a *minyan* for Sabbath and holiday services. The Baders, our nearest Jewish neighbors, who were seven miles away, could provide three of the required ten: Bader himself and two of his sons. We, of course, could furnish four, but that meant we still needed three more.

The absence of a *minyan* was hard enough on Sabbaths

and ordinary festivals, but on Rosh Hashona and Yom Kippur my father really suffered, and the rest of us suffered with him. The first Yom Kippur on the farm, when my father chanted the Kol Nidre to his family only, was a sad affair. The following year, regardless of the trouble and expense, my father traveled for Yom Kippur to the nearest town, taking my brothers along with him.

The third year brought a change. The Resnik family, with two grown sons, had bought the Campbell farm. It was six miles from us, but not in the same direction as the Bader's. The three farms were the points of a triangle, just about equally distant from one another. Now we had a *minyan,* and when the Holy Days came we worshiped together, the *minyan* passing regularly from one to the other.

In the year to which I refer it was the turn of the Baders. For weeks the weather had been bad, with heavy rains that turned the roads to mire and swelled the streams to floods. In the morning before Yom Kippur I took several boxes of eggs in our small cart to the village and came back with a number of purchases. I expected to be in time to accompany my parents and brothers in our big buggy to the Bader farmhouse, but when I returned they had already left. Ruth stood waiting for me at the wicket.

"It's late!" she cried. "The sun will be down before you get to the Baders."

The Kol Nidre service, you know, must begin just before sundown.

"I didn't waste any time," I explained, "but the roads are terrible."

"The road to the Baders is just as bad and it'll be dark before you get there," she replied.

The scene in the Bader parlor stood up vividy in my mind's eye. I saw the nine gazing towards the road and listening for the sound of hoofs and wheels. I saw my father's face grow more and more anxious. I saw my

mother peering between the curtains in the women's sec-
tion, directing mute questions to my father and brothers.
I dashed to the stable.

"I'll get there!" I cried. "Falcon will get me there!"
Falcon was our stallion and we all doted on him.

"See you tomorrow night!" I cried as I galloped past
Ruth. For the entire *minyan* would, of course, spend the
night and the following day at the Bader farmhouse.

My spirits were high and I felt confident. Is there anything more bracing than the rhythmic swing of a galloping
horse? The road was just mire, but it seemed to make no
difference to Falcon. I missed the drum of his hoofs, a
sound that is music to a rider, and I was sometimes splashed
with mud, but the distance to the Bader farm was being
swiftly sliced away.

I dashed through Campbell Corners, two miles from our
wicket. Old Jenkins, the hay-and-feed man, was on his
porch smoking his pipe placidly. He jumped to his feet as
I galloped past.

"Where to?" he shouted.

"To the *minyan*!" I shouted back and rode on. Our
Christian neighbors knew all about our *minyan*.

Another two miles would bring me to Salem Junction
which meant more than half the journey. Falcon showed
no signs of fatigue, but I judged it best to slow him to a trot.

At Salem Junction I had to stop for the five-fifteen
freight to clatter past. I knew it was a long train, but this
time it seemed endless.

"It's just as well, old boy," said I to Falcon. "You can
catch your breath."

I felt the animal quiver beneath me. He seemed to be
just as impatient as I was. "It wouldn't surprise me," I
told myself, "if he had some idea of where we are going."

Gus Williams, the station-master, whom people called
Gloomy Gus, came ambling towards us as we stood waiting
for that endless procession of boxcars to come to an end.

Gus was long and thin, with a mournful face that was always in motion. He was never without his quid.

"Where to?' he asked me.

"To the *minyan*," I told him.

"Bader's?"·

I nodded..

"Watch out," said Gus.

"Why?" I demanded.

Gus rolled his quid to the other side of his mouth and spat out.

"Been heavy rains 'round about here last couple weeks," said he, the words sounding like peas popping off a hot stove, and he ambled off

"That's Gloomy Gus," said I to Falcon, and the stallion came out with a brief neigh that sounded like a snort of disdain.

The freight came finally to an end, and we galloped away. I gave Falcon his head: we had to make up for the time we lost. In a little while, however, he changed to a trot.

"Getting tired?" said I. "Don't let me down, old boy."

A mile out of Salem Junction I came to a crossroad, and found myself facing a problem. I could continue up the main road and cross Clinton Creek by the iron bridge, or I could take a side road and cross by a wooden bridge, with the Bader farmhouse right there on the other side. The mud would be worse on the side road, but I would cut the distance by a good mile. There was no time to hesitate. I turned left and took the side road.

At once the stallion's legs sank more than half way to his knees, but he toiled on. The sun was now before me, and it seemed dangerously close to the horizon.

Falcon bore on bravely and at last we came to a pine wood which extended down to the creek. The path through the wood was a little better. Soon the creek would come in sight.

But before seeing the creek, I heard it. I heard it only too well. A vague fear swept over me. I slapped Falcon on the haunch and tried to shake it off.

In a few minutes we stood before the creek and I stared with amazement. The placid, bubbling little stream was a raging flood!

I turned the stallion's head toward the bridge, but suddenly I reined in. There was no bridge! I strained my eyes and saw jagged piles sticking up out of the flood. The old wooden bridge was gone!

I dismounted and stood staring at the spiky stumps. Never in my life had I seen anything so forlorn. Those broken piles symbolized all my despair. My throat tightened and a series of choking sounds gurgled out of it. I felt my face warm with a rush of tears.

The stallion whinnied. My hand was on his flank and I felt it quiver. I brought my arm around his mane and embraced him, as, I suppose, an unhappy child embraces a big brother.

"Falcon," I wept, "it's the end, the end of our journey!"

That horse understood me! I suppose you don't believe me, but I am sure he understood me. He arched his neck and neighed softly and briefly. And the sudden lift of his head had a strange effect on me.

"Falcon," I cried. "We'll do it, you and I!"

I was on his back in an instant and we made for the water. He stepped at once into the flood, and the next moment I felt the powerful beat of his strokes. I headed him aslant the current, so the rush of it wouldn't bear down on him directly.

I bent over and poured a flood of tender words into his ear. I was, I suppose, in a sort of delirium.

"Falcon, I love you," I sputtered. "You're the greatest that ever lived. You're a hero, a lion! And a pal, Falcon. You're a real pal, and I love you!"

A little beyond midstream his panting became more

A little beyond midstream his panting became more heavy

heavy. I slipped off the saddle and struck out beside him, and when I forged a little ahead I saw his big eyes look at me gratefully.

Well, I'm here telling you the story, which proves that I made it. We both made it. And when we staggered onto the bank I took the bridle and we toiled up to the Bader farmhouse. We had been forced a good distance downstream, and the way seemed endless. At last the house came into view. I shouted and Falcon followed with a shrill neigh.

Another minute and a dozen hands were in possession of us. They ripped the clothes off me and rubbed me till I begged for mercy.

"Who's taking care of Falcon?" I demanded.

"He's getting the same treatment," they answered.

They found some dry clothes for me, put a prayer shawl about my shoulders and led me into the parlor where the tiny congregation was assembled. My father was already at the lectern beside the little ark.

I looked through the window. The blood-red disk of the sun was still more than half way above the horizon.

A FOREST SEDER

The last strain of *Chad Gadya* rang out like a shout of triumph and the Seder was over. Our guests closed their Haggadot but were in no hurry to break up. The conversation became more and more lively. It was the effect, no doubt, of the good cheer and of the recital in song and story of the marvelous passage from slavery to freedom.

Gradually the talk turned on the subject of strange and unusual Sedarim. A number of such Sedarim were reported, of which I have only the vaguest recollection. One of them, however, has remained imbedded in my memory. The story was told by an elderly guest, and here it is as he told it.

It was still morning of the day before Passover, and in my little town in Russia every home was already spick-and-span and making last preparations for the first Seder to be celebrated that night. We did our best to dismiss from our thoughts the alarms and sorrows of the war, the First World War, already in its third year.

We knew, of course, that our town had been swept into the war zone. We knew the Germans were advancing and the town would soon be in their hands. But we tried to think of nothing but the joyous holiday that stood, so to speak, on our door-step. Spring had come in early that year and the bright sky above us seemed to share our joy.

From somewhere off to the east a troop of Cossacks came galloping and pulled up in front of the rabbi's house. The Cossack officer found the rabbi laying out the white linen robe which he was to wear at the Seder.

"Your people are to leave this town at once," he

ordered. "The enemy is advancing and you are being evacuated. You will take the road to Staromir and in two hours you will be on the way."

"But—but," the rabbi stammered, "it is Passover tonight —a holy festival—"

The Cossack whipped out his saber and held it aloft.

"In two hours!" he barked. "And whoever lags will get a taste of this!"

"But Staromir is thirteen miles from here," the rabbi pleaded. "With our women and children and baggage, how can we get there before nightfall when the festival begins?"

"Enough!" the Cossack snapped. "In two hours, beginning this minute! We will be your escort."

"It's the will of God," said the rabbi, and he sent off two messengers to convey the tidings to the people. But the news was already known. In some mysterious way it got around and people were already packing and preparing for exile.

To understand this brutal command you must remember that in the First World War the Russian armies suffered one defeat after another. The Czar's generals were bunglers and some of them were believed to be traitors. So they looked for a scapegoat on whom to lay the blame for their defeats and found it in the Jews, accusing them of giving aid to the enemy. Jewish communities, men, women and children, were uprooted and exiled to distant parts of the Russian empire, suffering cruel hardships on the way.

No matter what we had to leave behind, there was one thing none of us failed to take along: the unleavened bread. We took it hastily with us as, thousands of years ago, our ancestors had done in their flight from Egypt. Many found room also for the wine, the bitter herbs and other necessities they had prepared for the Seder.

We managed to secure a number of vehicles for the small children and very old, and we set out with half the Cossack troop riding before us and the other half bringing up the rear. They drove on those who lagged, shouting and cursing and sometimes swinging their knouts, which formed part of their equipment.

A mild spring day shone down on us and the road lay bright and yellow in the sunlight. On both sides the fields were freshly turned. We passed occasional clumps of trees whose branches were ready to burst into leaf.

But for all the nagging of our escort our progress was slow. The wagons were overloaded and moved with difficulty on the soft road. We had covered little more than half the distance to Staromir and the dusk was already creeping across the fields. When we entered the Byalin forest, five miles from our destination, we found ourselves quite in the dark.

In the forest we came to a halt. The rabbi implored the officer to let him conduct the Passover evening service, but the Cossack wouldn't hear of it. He was about to raise his voice in an angry command when a loud booming echoed through the forest. The Cossack stopped short. The first boom was followed by others, and from somewhere came a loud crash. A tree had been struck and blasted; somewhat in the forest the new life it held lay strewn in splinters.

The booming continued. Our Cossack vanguard and rearguard met and melted together, the little horses they sat on strangely calm beneath them. We heard the faint rustle of excited whispering, and occasionally a sudden cry, like the crack of a whip, escaped from the officer. Another crash reached our ears, this time a little nearer. A sharp command followed and the Cossacks reined about, galloped off and vanished.

The booming and crashing continued. A feeling of panic began coiling around us like a serpent. Mothers held their children more tightly, but the little ones continued to wail. Suddenly a loud and prolonged strain of song rose up above the din. At a signal from the rabbi the cantor had begun chanting the first words of the festival service. The effect of the sound was immediate and electric. It freed the people from the clutch of the gathering panic. At once they took up the chant.

We went through the service, joining the cantor even in those parts that belong to him alone. We seemed to be resolved that our praise of the Almighty should silence the thunder of the artillery.

The service ended. The rumble of the cannon could still be heard, but it seemed to have moved off into the distance.

"Let us," said the rabbi, "begin the Seder. Arrange yourselves in groups, families and neighbors together. Bring out the matzos, the wine and whatever else you have been able to take with you. And let us fear no one but Him, Who watches over us."

So the groups were formed and the Seder began. The Kiddush, chanted loud and in unison, echoed through the forest: .

"Blessed art Thou, O Lord, Our God, King of the Universe, Who has chosen us from all peoples, and exalted us above all tongues, and sanctified us by His commandments. And Thou has given us in love, O Lord our God, appointed times for gladness, festivals and seasons for joy, even this day of the Feast of Unleavened Bread, the season of our freedom . . ."

In due order and solemnity the celebration of the Seder continued. The four questions were asked and answered, the story of slavery and freedom retold, the meaning of the Passover sacrifice, the unleavened bread and bitter herbs expounded. And although the meal that followed was meager enough, consisting chiefly of the unleavened bread, our spirits rose even higher as we chanted the grace together.

The second half of the Seder began. We stood up to greet the prophet Elijah, but did not sit down again. Sounds reached our ears which held us rooted where we

The groups were formed and the Seder began

stood. They were trampling, crashing sounds and they seemed to come from every direction. Then, with the suddenness of a dream, a host of figures appeared and surrounded us. They were tall and dark, with bayonetted rifles and spiked helmets.

"The Germans! The Germans!" we whispered one to another.

One of them advanced and the rabbi stepped out to meet him.

"You will return where you came from!" the German announced.

"But we are much nearer to Staromir, where we can find rest for the night," the rabbi pleaded.

"Where you came from!" the German snapped.

"We have old people and small children. They are exhausted."

"You will start at once!" the German barked.

"Give us a little time to finish our Seder," the rabbi begged.

The German officer looked down with gloomy scorn at the bearded figure before him.

"Five minutes," he finally snarled.

The rabbi turned to us.

"We just have time to sing *Chad Gadya*," he said.

So we sang together the final song of the Seder. We began it timidly, but our voices gathered strength as we continued. The quaint parable of the victory of life over violence and death became our own song of triumph. The forest resounded with our last shout of *Chad Gadya*.

We began our return journey. We moved on in the dreamy moonlight like a dream procession, flanked on both sides by tall shadowy figures, with glinting helmets and bayonets.

Nevertheless, on this return journey our pace was faster. Where did we find our new vigor? No, not from the knowledge that we were going home. For we knew that our town was already in the hands of the enemy. It must have flowed from the strange Seder we celebrated that night in the embattled forest.

THE HOME-COMERS

There was a big party for Alvin Kane when he returned to Dayton, Ohio, from the war in the Pacific. The relatives were all there, of course, and leading men of the community, including the rabbi and cantor of the congregation, came to welcome him home.

His last letter was dated September 3, 1945. "Dear Mother and Dad," he wrote, "Yesterday I accepted the unconditional surrender of the Emperor Hirohito, the divine ruler of Japan. Please don't give me all the credit for it. There are quite a few other marines in my outfit who have put in a claim for it. I should be home soon, I hope. Will I be glad to put a soft fedora on my dome and get inside a pin stripe jacket and pants!"

Alvin spent the next few weeks looking up old friends and acquaintances and lounging through the streets of the town. Something was wrong. The thrill to which he looked forward after an absence of nearly four years shied away from him. People looked so much older, so tired. What made them so dull? And the houses and streets—how did they get so run-down and drab in such a short time?

"Son," said his father to him one day. "It's time we had a good talk. You were a sophomore at college when you enlisted. But you have no desire to go back and finish your studies and I am not going to insist on it. But have you given any thought to what you are going to do?"

"Not much, dad," Alvin grinned. "Four years of taking orders sort of unfits you for doing much thinking, I suppose."

"Well, son, I have a proposition for you," his father went on. "Come into the business with me. It's good and it promises to be even better. The wholesale grocery business is not as exciting as the jungles of the Pacific, but there is more future in it."

They both laughed and Alvin promised "to give it a whirl."

He tried. He really tried hard. He began by making the rounds of the customers: "getting acquainted with the trade," his father called it. But after two or three months of rattling through dingy streets and taking orders for hominy, jam and peanuts, he had enough.

"Dear Mother and Dad," ran the letter he left on his father's desk, "The change from the Pacific to groceries seems to have been too sudden. I just can't take it. I need something in between, and I'll look for it until I find it. Don't be too angry with me. I'll write and keep you posted."

For more than two years Alvin tried a variety of occupations. He was a keeper at a zoo, where he became especially fond of the big cats. It was a short step from the zoo to a traveling circus, but the blare and ballyhoo of this "show business" palled on him quickly. "Too much sham," he said to himself. "I have to have something real."

A chance acquaintance proposed he should join him in "a little scrap" as a soldier of fortune. Men were needed for "a revolution or something" that was being prepared in one of the smaller countries south of the border. The pay was excellent. Alvin felt a tug inside of him and said he would think it over.

"No," was his final answer. "If I am to shed blood, mine or someone else's, it must be for something I believe in—deeply."

"Sounds grand," said the other man, with the trace of a sneer in his voice.

"Look," Alvin told him, "I know I am a good deal of a gypsy, but there is still a lot of the Jew left in me."

"Oh," the other murmured. "So you are one of those, are you?"

Alvin stepped closer. "I am," he snapped. "You have something to say about it?"

"Oh, no!" was the prompt answer. "Not a word, not a word."

After a few more starts, all of them short-lived, Alvin signed on as a seaman on a tramp freighter and found at last something approaching inner contentment. This was real. The sea was always a challenge. In calm it glittered like a reptile. In storm it bounded and bellowed like a horde of stampeded steers. The ports at which his ships put in, each different from the others, swarmed with human beings, shouting, jostling and wrangling, all bent on something on which their very lives seemed to depend. Alvin felt strangely drawn towards them—and towards the ships also. It was a feeling not far removed from love.

After a number of voyages over the seven seas, with stops in every sizable port of the globe, he found himself one day on the water front of Baltimore, wondering if the time hadn't come to return to his kith and kin in Dayton. He felt a strange tugging at the heart, at once painful and precious. "Homesick, that's what I am," he confessed.

But suddenly his eye was caught by a peculiar craft moored to one of the docks. From stem to stern she seemed to be all cabin, from which the wheelhouse and stack were just visible. The only deck was just wide enough for two men to pass each other without colliding. Lifeboats hung close from their davits like a string of beads. The ship stood high along the pier and a board nailed just below the bulwarks bore the following message: "Able seamen wanted. Good pay, good food, good quarters. Apply on board."

Alvin's homesickness vanished. He stamped up the gangplank, and before he fully realized it he had signed on for another voyage.

"What sort of crazy tub is this?" he asked a crew mate. "She is not a freighter, and if she is going to take on passengers they won't be too cozy in those cubby holes. Just been clapped together, that's what they look like."

"Perhaps the passengers will not mind," the man replied slowly. His accent was clipped and he chose his words carefully. "There are people in the world today who are not very particular."

"Queer chap," thought Alvin. "Seems to have plenty of brawn, but he talks like a professor."

It was only after they were through the Strait of Gibraltar that Alvin learned what sort of ship he was on and where she was bound. The captain addressed the crew assembled in the forecastle. Beside him stood the man who spoke "like a professor."

"The captain," the man began, "will speak to you in his own language, which is Hebrew, and I will interpret."

The captain's speech was brief. "We are going to put in at Marseilles," he told the crew, "and there we will take on about 1,200 passengers, men, women and children. They are survivors of Nazi concentration camps where six million of their people were murdered. Our ship is ready for them. Some of you may already know she was remodeled from a coastal excursion ship. Our job will be to land our passengers on the coast of Palestine. It's not going to be easy. British destroyers are patrolling the shore, looking out for ships like ours. But we have word that Haganah, the Jewish underground, has blown up most of the British radar stations. That improves our chance of escaping capture. However, I am not asking you to stay on unless you want to. You may, if you wish, sign off at Marseilles. Your wages will be paid in full. That is all."

That night Alvin was kept awake by a strange excitement. Shreds of memories, scattered or tangled together, took on shape and meaning. He had fought the enemy in the Pacific: now he became sharply aware that he had really fought the enemy in Europe also. Those unhappy people waiting to be taken to Palestine—he had fought for them also.

He sat up suddenly in his berth. "My God!" he exclaimed. "They are my people, my own people!"

From the next berth came a sleepy voice. "Why don't you just pipe down?" it growled.

In the small hours of a black-velvet night the passengers slipped on board—noiselessly, almost stealthily. Without waiting for the dawn the ship weighed anchor and glided away eastward over the Mediterranean, the purr of her engines changing to a throb as she took on speed. A brilliant morning brought most of the passengers on deck, which soon became overcrowded. They were a sad lot, ragged, gaunt and hagard, these "brands plucked from the burning." Alvin looked at them and his throat tightened. A vast pity surged through him.

But before the morning was over he felt more than pity for them. It happened suddenly and swiftly. The "professor," who turned out to be the second mate, stationed him forward with orders to keep the approach to the pilot-house clear. A passenger approached, holding the hand of a small girl whom he seated near the companionway leading to the helm. Alvin performed a number of gestures to indicate that the man must find another place for the child.

"You want me to take her somewhere else," the man replied in surprisingly good English. "Where?"

"It sure is crowded," Avin agreed. "But my orders are to keep this space clear."

"She stays," the man declared curtly. "She needs the air, the sunshine. She stays."

"I'll find another place for her," said Alvin, bending down to lift the girl, who shrank away from him.

He staggered back before he could touch her. The man had seized him by the collar and flung him away.

Alvin was amazed. His opponent was lean and of less than average height. Where had he found the strength? But the challenge to combat was more than he could resist. He lunged at the man and threw him against the wheel-house. Then something happened that Alvin was never quite able to explain. He found himself hurtling through the air. He heard a loud splash and realized with surprise that it was he himself who had struck the sea.

The ship halted, its engines reversed and a life boat came bounding towards him. He pulled himself into it easily, none the worse for his ducking. In his bunk he put on a dry shirt and dungarees and sat awhile collecting his wits. He shrugged, grinned and laughed—softly at first then louder and louder. He thought of his lean and tough opponent, he thought of the others passengers. Pity? Yes. But now it was more than pity. It was admiration and, for some reason, pride also. "It's queer" he hold himself, "but I feel grateful for that ducking."

They met again the same day and promptly became friends. His name was Joshua. Just Joshua. When the Germans had wiped out his entire family, he gave up his family name. Besides, he explained, most family names of his people in Poland were of Polish or German origin. What did they want with such names? In Palestine he would choose himself a Hebrew name.

Before the war Joshua had taught modern languages in Warsaw, and he had managed to live through the agonies and terrors which the Germans inflicted on the Jews in the Warsaw Ghetto. In the final uprising against the Nazis he was in command of one of the cellar bunkers. When that last blaze of rebellion was quenched by German tanks, flamethrowers and bombers, he was one of a small number who escaped from the burning ruins through the Warsaw sewer. He fled to the forests where he found a unit of Jewish guerrillas and joined them.

"And there, I suppose, you learned the trick that sent me splashing into the Mediterranean," Alvin laughed.

"That one and a few more," Joshua admitted.

As for the little girl, five years ago, when she was only six, he had found her living with a Polish family in a village on the edge of the forest. Her parents had left her with the Poles, together with a generous sum of money, to protect her from the Germans. But the protectors began to fear for their own lives. Spiteful neighbors might inform.

"We formed rings and danced the hora."

on them and the Germans would kill them also. Joshua felt uneasy. He suspected they might do away with the child, so he took her with him and for two years she lived with the partisans in their forest hide-outs. Nor was she the only child who found refuge with them. Now, Joshua concluded with a broad grin, she intended to marry him.

The ship, all of whose passengers could have told similar stories of suffering and peril, moved on warily towards the Promised Land. In the late afternoon of the fifth day, through a mist that came down from a blustery sky, a dim line became visible. Where were the British destroyers? It was mid-May of the year 1948. Had the warships become less watchful? Or did they fail to receive the signals they needed from their radar stations on the coast?

*

A month or so later the Kanes in Dayton, Ohio, took from their mailbox a letter for which they had long been waiting. "It's a nice long letter," said Mrs. Kane when she opened it. "Alvin must have a twinge of conscience. It wouldn't surprise me if he is on the way home." And she read it to her husband.

"Dear Mother and Dad: Did you have a good look at the postmark? Look at it again. It's from Israel, the State of Israel! You read about it, but I'm right in it. And let me tell you I've never been any place so wonderful and exciting in my life.

"How did I get here? In a crazy old tub fitted up in Baltimore and jampacked with refugees in Marseilles. We got by the British, but just as we hove in to shore we ran smack into a heavy storm. But they waited for us, I mean the Haganah boys, and every one of us was safely landed. Some of us got a ducking, including your everloving son. But that was the second ducking I got on this trip. Some other time I'll tell you about the first.

"On shore there were trucks waiting to take us to different settlements. I say us because I feel I am one of them. Why? Well, it's not easy to put it in words. They suffered more cruelly than any other people in the world. And what were they guilty of? The same crime of which I am guilty. I am also a Jew.

"But we were in no hurry to get into the trucks. They told us that the same afternoon the State of Israel had been proclaimed. The whole lot of us went wild with joy. We formed rings and danced and shouted like mad. The hora, that's what the dance is called, and it's a sure cure for a slow circulation.

"But I know what you are thinking. So why isn't he on the way home? you are asking. Well, there is a little unfinished business here. You must have read about it. The neighbors all around us are not too happy with the newborn infant. I mean, of course, the new State. They are out to strangle it. But they'll have to do a lot better than they have been doing. I don't think they stand a chance. I am helping a little to finish what they began. Didn't I graduate from the best finishing school in Iwo Jima? I am in the same unit as my friend Joshua, the chap who gave me that first ducking. He came here with a little girl friend, who is now living in a children's village.

"I could go on and on, but the guy who collects the mail is breathing down my neck and I must wind up. So here is another salute from your prodigal son—and from Israel."

ACKNOWLEDGMENTS

*For the general idea underlying this sheaf
of stories the author is indebted
to the late Dr. Samson Benderly;
and he is grateful to
Dr. Abraham E. Milgram for supplying
the impulse to bring
the idea to fruition.*